Baltimore & Ohio
RAILROAD

Kirk Reynolds and David P. Oroszi

MBI Publishing Company

First published in 2000 by MBI Publishing Company, PO Box 1, 729 Prospect Avenue, Osceola, WI 54020-0001 USA

© Andover Junction Publications, 2000

Book design and layout by Mike Schafer and Maureene D. Gulbrandsen/Andover Junction Publications, Blairstown, New Jersey, and Lee, Illinois.

Edited by Mike Schafer/Andover Junction Publications

MBI Publishing Company books are also available at discounts in bulk quantity for industrial or sales-promotional use. For details write to Special Sales Manager at Motorbooks International Wholesalers & Distributors, 729 Prospect Avenue, PO Box 1, Osceola WI, 54020-0001 USA.

Library of Congress Cataloging-in-Publication Data Available
ISBN 0-7603-0746-6

On the front cover: A gentle June rain washes the Electro-Motive passenger diesels idling away at the head end of the eastbound *Shenandoah* about to depart Chicago's Grand Central Station in 1964. The *Shenandoah* provided overnight service between Chicago and Pittsburgh and day service across the Alleghenies between Pittsburgh and Washington. *Jim Boyd*

On the frontispiece: An ornate glass sign from the early twentieth century harkens to an era when even such simple things as signage took on an art form. *Howard Ameling*

On the title page: The eastbound *Capitol Limited* brakes for its station stop at La Paz, Indiana, on a late summer's evening in 1970. *Mike Schafer*

On the back cover: Two B&O Electro-Motive E6 passenger diesel locomotives, photographed at St. Louis Station in 1965, have ushered the Washington–St. Louis *Metropolitan* into town and are being shuttled off to the locomotive servicing facility. *Jim Boyd*

Printed in China

B&O CONTENTS

ACKNOWLEDGMENTS

The history of the Baltimore & Ohio Railroad is a tale of daring initiative, unprecedented mechanical innovation, missed opportunities, and a lot of hard work on the part of B&O's workforce and management. It is most fortunate so much of the history and tradition of America's oldest common carrier railroad is preserved into the twenty-first century.

Although many books and other publications have been produced covering the many aspects of the B&O, the purpose of this volume is to present a general review of the Baltimore & Ohio story. Many individuals were involved in the creation of this work. We are fortunate to have had access to many sources of B&O historical material and are most indebted to those who helped us to make this book possible.

Sincere thanks go to Herbert H. Harwood Jr. and William F. Howes Jr. for their generosity in providing photos, company literature, and vital B&O information. They were also kind enough to take the time to review our manuscript. We also wish to express our deep gratitude to David Ori, Mark Perri, and Stephen Salamon for providing essential data detailing Baltimore & Ohio operations and for helping with the preparation of the book's text.

Since this is also a picture book, we give special recognition to the almost two dozen photographers whose works appear in these pages. They include R. D. Acton Sr., Howard Ameling, John P. Baukus Jr., Thomas A. Biery, Jim Boyd, Harold Buckley Jr., James V Claflin, William T. Clynes, Cliff Comer, Ken Douglas, Jim Edmonston, Dan Finfrock, Hank Goerke, Herbert H. Harwood Jr., Dave Ingles, Robert S. Kaplan, Louis A. Marre, Bradley McClelland, Brian McDowell, William Myers, Dennis Nehrenz, Jim O'Dell, Dave Ori, Joseph Oroszi, W.R. Osborne Mark Perri, Steve Salamon, Mike Schafer, Alvin Schultze, Ray Thibault, and Don Woodworth Jr.

Most importantly, we wish to thank our wives, Jill Oroszi and Toni Reynolds, for their support and patience throughout this project.

David P. Oroszi
Kirk Reynolds
June, 1999

Wearing the cherished blue, gray, and black livery, a set of Electro-Motive F-units charge through Lima, Ohio, on a late summer's afternoon in 1960 with a freight bound for Toledo, Ohio. *Dave Ingles*

While the Baltimore & Ohio Railroad no longer survives as the nation's oldest railroad, its legacy endures. As an upstart corporate youngster, the B&O challenged convention, legend says, racing a team of horses with its locomotive, the *Tom Thumb*. As an adolescent, the B&O prospered, growing through merger, acquisition, and construction to support America's industrial heartland. As the railroad matured, competitive and external forces took their toll, and the B&O began to fade into the background as a "sister" railroad to the more prosperous and stronger C&O, as a partner in the Chessie System, and into corporate dissolution as a component of CSX.

From its beginnings in 1827, the fledgling B&O was an integral part of our young nation's expansion, when "the West" meant the Ohio River. Reliable, all-weather transportation now connected the East Coast with the Ohio Valley. Through the Civil War years, the B&O was both a lifeline and a target. To this day, a stone-arch bridge which spans the Potomac River still bears scars of a cannon bombardment, yet continues to support the main line and its trains on the torturous Seventeen-Mile Grade.

The early 1900s were the years of growth, and by 1927 the B&O celebrated 100 years and was now "Linking 13 Great States with the Nation." The B&O dieselized with style. Slant-nosed EA No. 51, delivered in 1937, began a relationship with builder Electro-Motive that would endure for decades . . . and would set a standard for passenger power, epitomized by a group of F3s delivered in 1947. Geared for passenger speeds, equipped with steam boilers, modified with streamlined pilots, and dressed in the most intricate version of B&O's blue, gray, and yellow paint schemes, they were a visual icon of B&O in its finest hour. (The first actual passenger diesel was No. 50 purchased from EMC in 1935, which had a box-cab design.)

Even through the post-World War II "Golden Years" of passenger and freight railroading, B&O increasingly became the underdog. Physically, the B&O fought daily to wrestle tonnage over the Alleghenies, and, corporately, B&O was always a scrappy competitor. But the B&O was not blessed with the dominating size of the Pennsy, the relentless wealth of the Norfolk & Western, or even the Madison Avenue image of the New York Central, and soon, the interstate system and airlines began to take their toll.

What B&O did have though, from the executive suite to the tie gang, was an inner pride, and a railroader's attitude . . . the B&O had character. Even under increasingly larger corporate umbrellas, B&O operated with some autonomy. While the C&O dabbled in locomotives from General Electric, B&O remained a devoted customer of Electro-Motive. Seven years into the Chessie System merger, Cumberland Shops performed major modifications, in house, to a group of older Electro-Motive SD35s for use in hump yards. When the first "SD20–2" was outshopped for testing, it wore a fresh coat of royal blue paint with B&O lettering. Into the 1980s, most freights were named. Even though to some a train name may not mean much, couldn't an engineer, an operator, or a maintainer take some pride in the expeditious handling of trains like the *Allegheny*, the *Queen City Flyer*, or the *Baltimore Clipper*, instead of just another train identified by a clumsy amalgamation of abbreviations?

It's human nature to wonder "what if," in the late 1990s, our beloved B&O still existed? Often, as vestiges of the B&O disappear, we lament the loss of familiar paint schemes, operations, and practices of days gone by. Gently folded into the Chessie System in 1972 and absorbed by CSX in 1987, could we predict what a modern-day B&O, in a perfect world, would look like?

Being the pioneering, progressive, and proud railroad that we would expect, would this modern-day B&O certainly have purchased a fleet of luxurious Superliner coaches, diners, sleepers, and lounges—not unlike Amtrak's *Capitol Limited*, which plies the B&O daily? Would this B&O of the 1990s have gone to EMD for its latest power, not unlike the burly SD70MACs which now move West Virginia coal east through Cumberland? And would not the treasured royal blue give way to a modern B&O image, not unlike the familiar blue, gray, and yellow which adorns today's CSX locomotives?

Even as the remaining visible, obvious physical signs of the B&O are rapidly disappearing in the late 1990s, its legacy, those intangible practices and traditions of days when class and character meant something, always seem to surface and remind us of a railroad past.

Mark Perri
Akron, Ohio
May 1999

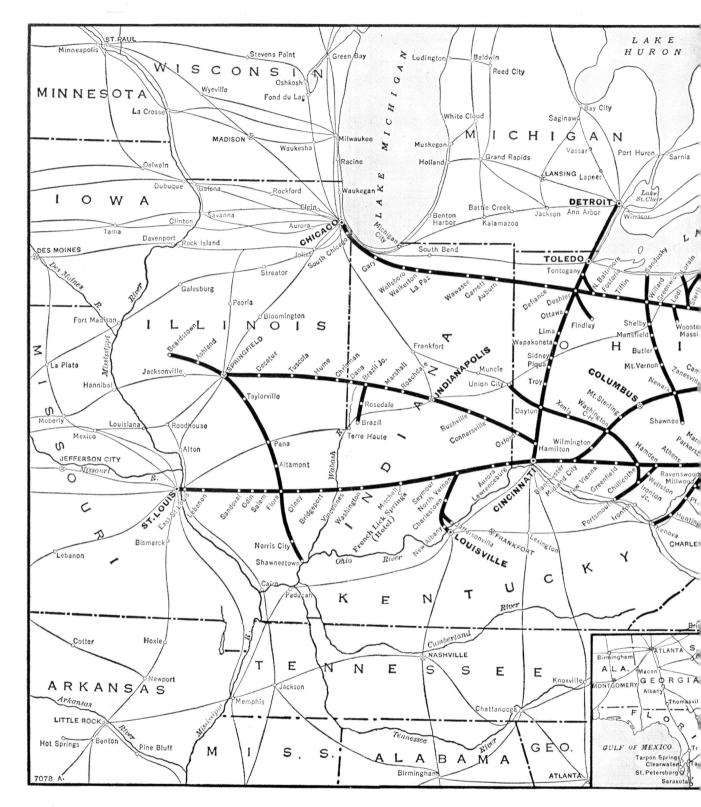

A map from a 1954 B&O public passenger timetable shows the railroad nearly at its peak. The branches to Wellsville and Addison in southern New York State have already been isolated by the abandonment of service between Burrows and Sinnemahoning in northern Pennsylvania. Operation of the isolated lines would eventually be transferred to shortline Wellsville, Addison & Galeton Railroad. A number of mining spurs in West Virginia had also been abandoned by this time as had a number of short spurs off the former Buffalo, Rochester & Pittsburgh main line between Butler and Ridgeway, Pennsylvania.

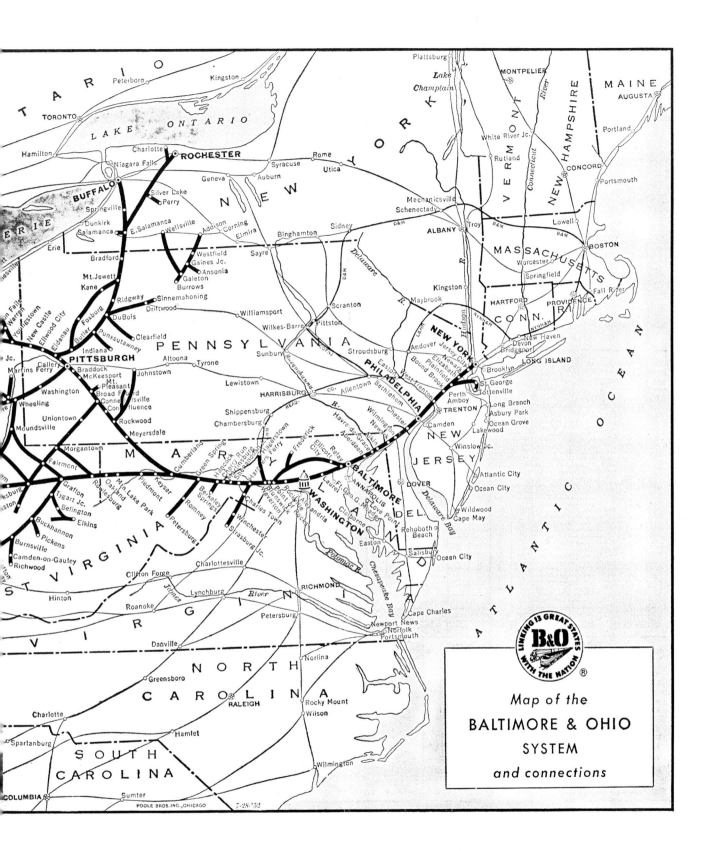

Map of the
BALTIMORE & OHIO
SYSTEM
and connections

LINKING 13 GREAT STATES
B&O
WITH THE NATION

POOLE BROS. INC., CHICAGO   7-28-'52

9

The B&O insignia is the crown jewel on the depot and office building at Grafton, West Virginia, in September 1982. The building was an imposing, ornate, three-story structure that stood on the north side of the Grafton yard complex. It not only housed passenger station facilities, but also division offices. For years Grafton was a crew-change point on the B&O. *Ray Thibaut*

CHAPTER 1

Birth of the Baltimore & Ohio

AMERICA'S FIRST COMMON-CARRIER RAILROAD: 1828–1865

In the early 1800s, the United States was a young, growing republic. Although most of America's population lived in the Atlantic coastal states, the 1803 Louisiana Purchase created a nation that stretched from Canada to the Gulf of Mexico and reached as far west as the Rocky Mountains. Between the Eastern states and the untamed interior stood the Appalachian Mountains. Frontiersmen had begun crossing the mountain chain before the Revolutionary War, and colonial and English capitalists established land companies to speculate the Western territories.

After the end of the Revolutionary War, the land beyond the Appalachians drew many settlers, and three new states joined the original 13: Kentucky in 1792, Tennessee in 1796, and Ohio in 1803. The westward tide of migration increased dramatically. Since there were few land routes to the region, many of these settlers traveled by flatboat down the Ohio River and its tributaries.

During the first 30 years of the nineteenth century, the most prominent American seaports on the East Coast were Boston, New York, Philadelphia, Baltimore, and Charleston, South Carolina. Boston was at a disadvantage by being located farther east of the new states, and Charleston was much farther south on the Atlantic coast. Thus, New York, Philadelphia, and Baltimore were best situated to reach inland toward the expanding Middle West.

By 1825, five more states had been admitted to the Union: Indiana, Mississippi, Illinois, Alabama, and Missouri. By that time, New York had surpassed Philadelphia and Baltimore in terms of international trade and was about to gain a major advantage in trade to what would become the Middle West (at the time, simply referred to as the "West") with the completion of the Erie Canal. Stretching 364 miles from Albany, on the Hudson River, to Buffalo, on Lake Erie, the Erie Canal gave the New York City an unrivaled route to the Great Lakes. Philadelphia and Baltimore had to find new routes to the West or they would wither and perish.

Pennsylvania had well over 2,000 miles of turnpikes (toll roads in today's terms) in the early 1820s, and over half of that mileage was hard surfaced—an impressive percentage in those days. However, the amount of horsepower required to move a ton of cargo by Conestoga wagon over those improved roads was several times more than that required by a canal boat, in part because of the rugged geography of Pennsylvania.

Opened in 1825, New York's Erie Canal had been built over terrain that was far more level than that of the Commonwealth of Pennsylvania. Eager to compete with the Erie Canal, the Pennsylvania legislature sought a means of transport that could carry more freight per horsepower over the mountains to Pittsburgh, but realized that there was no practical way of building a canal across the Alleghenies. Instead, the State sponsored the construction of a system that was a peculiar combination of canals, railroads, and inclined planes.

Construction of Pennsylvania's Main Line of Public Works began on July 4, 1826, and was completed in 1834. Its operation portended —albeit a mite clumsily—intermodal transport. Special vessels resembling three-section canal boats were carried on special railway flat cars. When the train reached a canal segment, the special vessels were lowered into the water and moved along the waterways. Likewise, when they reached the base of an incline plane, they were separated, loaded onto cable cars, hoisted over the summit of the mountain range, and reassembled to continue as canal boats again. Obviously, this was a time-consuming arrangement and, in the long run, the Main Line Canal failed financially to meet the expectations of its sponsors.

By 1825, Baltimore was a thriving city possessing many commercial assets. Located at the northern end of Chesapeake Bay, it had a fine harbor and was farther inland than its rival seaports, New York and Philadelphia. A vigorous shipping trade had been established out of its port, and a network of roads radiated from the city to connect with the surrounding area. In addition, the federal government had passed legislation in 1806 to build the National Road (also known as the Cumberland Road) from Cumberland, Maryland, to Wheeling, Virginia (later, West Virginia), on the Ohio River. Upon its completion in 1818, the National Road was one the best roads of its time and provided Baltimore access to the Ohio Valley.

Nonetheless, the citizens and business community of Baltimore watched with concern as the Erie Canal gave New York City the upper hand in the competition for trade with the Western states. The start of Pennsylvania's MLofPW route to Pittsburgh likewise spurred apprehension. Baltimoreans realized that their city needed its own improved transportation route to the West if it was to keep pace with New York and Philadelphia. The most likely destination of such a passage would be some point on the Ohio River where travelers and cargo could transfer to steamboats.

The geography of Maryland, like Pennsylvania, is rugged and bound by the Appalachians to the west, and therefore a canal was not a practical solution. And as good as the National Road was, teams of four or six horses were required to move a Conestoga wagon over the turnpike. The freight rates charged by then-thriving canals such as the Erie were much lower than those that could be offered by wagons, even on the best roads. Baltimore had to find a better way to move people and goods over the mountains.

BALTIMORE BUILDS A RAILROAD

In England early in the 1800s, a new mode of transportation called the railway was being developed. Horse-drawn wagons riding on iron rails had been hauling coal from mines and stone from quarries since it was discovered that a horse pulling a wagon on rails could move a much greater load than it could with a wagon on a paved road. In 1804, Richard Trevithick advanced railway technology by a leap when he built and demonstrated the first steam locomotive. The world's first public railway, the Stockton & Darlington, opened in 1825, the same year the Erie Canal went into operation.

It was about this time that a group of Baltimore businessmen were looking for a better means of conveyance from Baltimore to the Ohio River. Baltimore bankers Phillip E. Thomas, Alexander Brown, and merchant William Patterson had heard accounts of the new railways in England from Thomas's brother, Evan, and Brown's oldest son, William, both of whom had inspected the Stockton & Darlington firsthand. As their discussions on the matter progressed, they concluded that a canal to the Ohio River was not a workable alternative to the existing turnpikes. By February 1827, the group began to seriously consider constructing a railway instead.

To make such a decision at that time was something of a leap of faith. Roads and canals were time-proven means of travel, but railroads were pretty much an unknown quantity. Although the S&D had been in operation for two years, that line was essentially a tramway built to haul coal from a mine. The sum of experience in the infant field of rail transport was very limited, and the Baltimore committee drew most of its conclusions from observing this very earliest example of railroading.

John Van Leer McMahon, a Baltimore lawyer who was also a member of the Maryland House of Delegates, prepared a charter for Baltimore & Ohio Railroad. When he presented the landmark charter to the Maryland legislature on February 28, 1827, the assembly approved it. The charter had authorized the project to be capitalized through sale of stock at $3 million but allowed the company to sell more stock if the board of directors thought it necessary. On April 23, 1827, twelve prominent Baltimore businessmen were elected to the first board of directors of the Baltimore & Ohio Railroad, and the railroad was organized and incorporated the following day. Phillip E. Thomas was voted in as B&O's first president.

Survey of a route for the B&O began in July 1827 under the direction of Lt. Col. Stephen H. Long of the United States Army and Jonathan

This painting by Stanley M. Arthurs depicts the ceremonies held on July 4, 1828, in Baltimore to celebrate the start of construction of the B&O. The first spade of earth was turned by the last surviving signer of the Declaration of Independence, Charles Carroll.
B&O photo, collection of William F. Howes Jr.

Knight, a civil engineer who had been involved in the construction of the National Road as well as turnpikes in Pennsylvania.

B&O's board of directors had planned to begin service with small horse-drawn cars but hoped to eventually use steam locomotives for propulsion. The capabilities of steam traction were even more vague than those of railways in general during those early days, so Long and Knight had to guess at what the maximum curvature and grade of the proposed right-of-way should be. They decided to restrict the ruling grade to a conservative 0.6 percent but allowed the curves to be rather tight at 14-18 degrees. (As reality would later reveal, steam locomotives would be able to handle steeper grades but needed wider curves.)

The surveyors planned for the railroad to follow the Potomac River Valley to Cumberland before crossing the Allegheny Mountains, but the first hurdle was reaching the Potomac River from Baltimore. It was decided to build along the Patapsco River to Parrs Ridge, which the railroad would cross, and continue down the Monocacy River Valley before reaching the Potomac near Harpers Ferry. The logical path for B&O would be to run southward along the edge of the harbor to the point where the Patapsco flowed into Chesapeake Bay and then follow the river inland. However, when the city of Baltimore agreed to purchase $500,000 of stock in B&O, the city stipulated that the railroad enter the city at an elevation of 66 feet. This provision was intended to prevent the B&O from contributing to economic development along the harbor south of Baltimore, but created many problems for the railroad when it built westward from the city.

When the route to Cumberland had been laid out and the directors determined that sufficient funding had been secured, the B&O was ready to begin construction. It had become a tradition to commemorate the start of new canal construction on Independence Day, and since the B&O was no less ambitious than any canal, a grand parade and special ceremonies were held on July 4, 1828. The first spade of earth was turned by the last surviving signer of the Declaration of Independence, Charles Carroll, and on that day the cornerstone—which still exists—of the B&O was laid.

Bids for construction for the first 12 miles of the line were taken through August and B&O's board of engineers went to England in November to see the Stockton & Darlington as well as another line still under construction,

A comparison of original wood-stringer strap rail with modern "T" rail. Track structuring was still in the experimental stage when the B&O first started construction. Railroad builders tried a number of methods, and iron strap rail mounted on wood beams mounted on wood ties worked best—until the current-day T-rail came into widespread use. *Herbert H. Harwood Jr.*

the Liverpool & Manchester. From the experience gained on this expedition, they recommended that the B&O adopt the English track gauge of 4 feet, 8 1/2 inches—today's standard gauge.

Grading of the right-of-way and construction of the first stone viaducts were done during the winter of 1828–29 and the first track was laid in 1829. Track structure was still in the experimental stage at that point, and several variations were tried. Each method involved laying strap iron along a supporting structure, as rolled iron rails were only available from England and were very expensive. One method involved laying the iron straps on stone sills running longitudinally, while a similar design used wooden beams (or "stringers") mounted on stone blocks. Another technique involved laying the iron straps along wooden

beams that were held in place with wooden crossties. This third method turned out to be the most satisfactory and economical for B&O. Each of these early track structures had an earth path between the rails to accommodate the horses that powered the first B&O trains.

With about a mile and a half of track in place by January 1830, B&O began carrying passengers for a nominal fare and generated its first revenues. In May of that year, the B&O became the first American railroad to offer scheduled passenger service when it completed 13 miles of line from the station at Pratt Street in Baltimore to Ellicotts Mills. These early passenger trains consisted of one or more rail-wagons drawn by a single horse.

During the summer of 1830, the railroad tested its first steam locomotive, later called the *Tom Thumb*. The small one-ton engine was an experiment and is probably most often remembered for losing a race with a horse. In reality, it proved to B&O directors that a steam locomotive was more powerful and dependable than any horse.

The railroad pushed westward along the Patapsco River valley until it reached the base of Parrs Ridge, about 40 miles west of Baltimore, by the middle of 1831. The ridge presented B&O engineers with their first major obstruction, separating the Patapsco valley from the projected route of the railroad along Bush Creek on the opposite side of the crest. Working with little practical experience in railway construction, the engineering staff decided to cross the ridge with a series of inclined planes, two on the eastern side and two on the western slope. Trains negotiating the inclines required additional horses, and the placement of stationary steam hoists was planned to eventually supplant horses on the inclines.

B&O's directors had been encouraged by their experience with the *Tom Thumb* and in January 1831 announced that the railroad would hold a contest for new steam locomotive designs. Five entries were submitted, and the winning design was a 3 1/2-ton machine

A replica of the *Tom Thumb* was built for the 1927 Fair of the Iron Horse. *Tom Thumb* was the first steam locomotive used by the B&O, in 1830. Though most often remembered for losing a race with a horse, the *Tom Thumb* proved to B&O directors that steam power was more powerful and dependable than real horsepower. *Collection of William F. Howes Jr.*

named *York* with an 0-4-0 wheel arrangement, built by Phineas Davis of York, Pennsylvania. Although the *York* was eventually found to be unsatisfactory in regular service and retired about a year later, steam power had become the mainstay of B&O's motive-power policy.

Phineas Davis completed B&O's second locomotive (the *Tom Thumb* was regarded only as an experiment) at Mount Clare in September 1832. The Atlantic weighed 6½ tons, had a 2-2-0 wheel arrangement, and, like the *Tom Thumb* and the *York*, had a vertical boiler. The Atlantic's performance was an improvement over that of the *York*, and a similar locomotive, named *Traveler*, was put in service about a year later. Owing to their vertical cylinders and drive rods, these engines were dubbed "Grasshoppers," and their design was gradually refined through the 1830s. The Grasshoppers became B&O's standard locomotive until the arrival of the first horizontal-boilered engine, the *Lafayette*, in 1837.

With the completion of the Parrs Ridge inclines, B&O came down to Bush Creek and crossed the Monocacy River on a three-span

wood deck-truss bridge. B&O's first branch split from the main line at the western end of the bridge and ran northward 3.5 miles to Frederick, Maryland. A good portion of the initial financial support for B&O had come from Frederick, as many of its citizens had assumed the line would pass through their city. However, the better route lay a few miles south along the valley of Bush Creek, and it was decided to build the main line along the easier grade and instead serve Frederick off a branch—the first branchline in American railroading. Train service to Frederick began in December 1831.

Construction of the B&O continued westward from the Monocacy River, and the line was completed to the Potomac River at Point of Rocks, Maryland, on April 1832. Not long afterward, a brief dispute arose over how B&O and the Chesapeake & Ohio Canal would share the same bank of the Potomac between Point of Rocks and Harpers Ferry. The Maryland legislature mediated a settlement between the railroad and the canal, and the B&O was able to finish its line to Harpers Ferry in December 1834. Under the terms of the settlement, however,

The depot at Ellicott City, Maryland—probably built in the fall of 1831—was one of the first permanent structures on the railroad. This view of an eastbound heading for Baltimore was taken in the 1890s. *B&O Railroad Museum*

15

A B&O suburban train approaches Point of Rocks, Maryland, on a lazy summer evening in 1979. The line in the foreground of the depot was completed between Baltimore and Point of Rocks in April 1832, while that which the passenger train rides is the old Metropolitan Branch from Washington, D.C. This Washington line was completed in 1873, and the depot—one of the most photographed small-town depots in the U.S.—was built circa 1875. In later years most rail traffic went via Washington, and the line to the left became known as the Old Main Line. Today, MARC (Maryland Rail Commuter) suburban trains still call at the picturesque structure, and Amtrak *Capitol Limited* passengers can briefly view the building as the train cruises by twice daily. *Mike Schafer*

B&O was unable to build farther west along its originally planned route following the north bank of the Potomac River. It had to find a new route to Cumberland through Virginia.

As the construction gangs built the main line toward Harpers Ferry, the B&O was planning its second branch, a 32-mile line to Washington, D.C. The first $500,000 of stock to build the Washington branch was purchased by the State of Maryland under the conditions that two more state directors be added to B&O's board and a 20 percent tax, derived from the branch's revenues, paid to the state.

Work on the branch began in October 1833.

The new line branched south from the main line at Relay, about 7^1/$_2$ miles west of Pratt Street. Track structure was much different from that on the main line, as rolled iron "T" rails replaced strap iron on wooden stringers supported by wooden crossties; no stone support was employed. Service on the branch began on August 25, 1835.

In December 1834, the third Grasshopper delivered to B&O, the *Arabian*, was running eastbound from Harpers Ferry with a two-car train when it successfully climbed the inclined planes at Parrs Ridge unassisted. By March 1836 there were several improved locomotives based on the Grasshopper design at work on the B&O, and on March 22 the *Andrew Jackson* conquered the ridge while pulling its four-wheel tender and a loaded eight-wheel car. From this point on, B&O's engineering staff realized that their steam locomotives could negotiate Parrs Ridge and began work to realign the track over the summit, eliminating the inclined planes.

A change in B&O leadership came on June 30, 1836, when President Phillip Thomas stepped down for health and personal reasons. Upon learning of his impending resignation, the B&O board of directors began looking for a replacement and elected Joseph W. Patterson to the position temporarily. Patterson was the son of one of B&O's original directors, William Patterson, and joined the board after his father's death in the spring of 1835.

This was a desperate time for B&O. Much of the money that had been raised to build the railroad to the Ohio River had been spent, and the B&O hadn't even reached Cumberland. Actual construction costs had been much higher than original estimates, partly due to unproven methods of building track and the extensive use of stone viaducts. Revenues had fallen far short of the projections made by B&O's proponents when the railroad was being planned. B&O needed the leadership of someone who could maintain the backing of its biggest benefactors, Baltimore and Maryland, as well as European investors, in order to drive construction of the line to its destination on the Ohio River.

ACROSS THE ALLEGHENIES

On December 27, 1836, Louis McLane was elected as the B&O's third president. He had a lengthy career in public service, first as a congressman from Delaware (1817–1829) and then as a member of Andrew Jackson's cabinet (1829–1834). As president of the Morris Canal & Banking Company, B&O's board of directors regarded McLane as a man who could finish building the railroad to its goal.

THE CAPITOL LIMITED—ALONG THE POTOMAC RIVER—BALTIMORE & OHIO RAILROAD

When he came to B&O, McLane took charge of a railroad that was in sad shape, as much of the eastern end of line needed to be rebuilt. The stone sill and wrought iron strap track structure that made up much of the line on the earliest segments of the B&O was falling apart. The iron T-rail on the Washington branch had proven to B&O engineers that it had many advantages.

The reconstruction of the B&O over Parrs Ridge was partially accomplished with T-rail while some of the new line was built with recycled strap iron laid on wooden stringers. At the same time, portions of the eastern end of the B&O were being rebuilt with new rolled iron rail. Given the financial status of the railroad at the time, only some sections of track could receive new rail while other parts would be rebuilt with the best of the recovered strap iron. Fortunately for the B&O, the Grasshoppers were at home on either type of rail— much of the railroad from Baltimore to Harpers Ferry would not be rebuilt with new rail until the late 1840s.

Of foremost importance to President McLane and his railroad was securing the money to finish building to the Ohio River or at least (for the time being) to Cumberland. The City of Baltimore and the State of Maryland had each pledged to purchase another $3 million in B&O stock in the summer of 1836, but an economic recession from 1838 through 1840 delayed the funding promised by Baltimore.

Between Point of Rocks and Harpers Ferry, the B&O and the Chesapeake & Ohio Canal shared the same bank of the Potomac River. This section of the B&O was completed in December 1834 and is depicted in this postcard issued early in the twentieth century. *Collection of William F. Howes Jr.*

B&O's Bollman truss-span bridge built in 1837 across the Potomac River at Harpers Ferry is shown circa 1870 in a view that looks west from Maryland. The line to the right was a short freight spur. *B&O Railroad Museum*

Mr. McLane traveled to England seeking financial backing for the B&O and was able to obtain sufficient funding to continue construction to Cumberland.

The B&O built a bridge across the Potomac at Harpers Ferry in January 1837 to connect with the recently completed Winchester & Potomac Railroad. When construction of the line to Cumberland began in 1839, the south end of the bridge had to be rebuilt to accommodate the new line, as the structure had orig-

inally been built to align with the tracks of W&P which ran along the Shenandoah River. The junction for the track to Cumberland was located on the bridge, and a new span carried the Cumberland line as it curved toward the Virginia side of the Potomac River.

As constructed, the Cumberland line left the Potomac Valley for several miles, cutting cross country though Martinsburg before returning to the river across from Hancock, Maryland. From there, B&O continued along

B&O's depot and Queen City Hotel at the railroad's important junction point of Cumberland, Maryland, was a landmark. Unfortunately, the structure was torn down in the 1970s after the (temporary) elimination of passenger service, but was still standing in March 1971 when this photo was taken. *Thomas A. Biery*

the south bank of the Potomac for about 50 miles and crossed the river back to Maryland at North Branch. The railroad was completed to Cumberland, a few miles beyond the bridge, on November 5, 1842. Cumberland was 178 miles west of Baltimore and about halfway to the Ohio River at Wheeling, Virginia.

The McLane administration continued to rebuild the railroad and put new locomotives and rolling stock in service during the 1840s. Revenues rose through the decade as the B&O moved increasing amounts of coal, and the company's stock actually paid small dividends. But the B&O was facing competition from other railroads. During the 1840s, several railroads linked up across the State of New York to form a speedy alternative to the Erie Canal that would eventually become the New York Central. Another line, the Erie Railroad, was building its tracks across the southern part of the Empire State. Also, the Pennsylvania Railroad was under construction between Harrisburg and Pittsburgh.

By 1848, B&O had not made any westward progress in six years, and its private stockholders, as well as the City of Baltimore and the State of Maryland, were anxious to see their railroad completed to the Ohio River. Louis McLane resigned from his position October 9, 1848, and on October 11 Thomas

Swann became B&O's fourth president.

The B&O of which Mr. Swann had taken charge was in much better condition than the B&O that Mr. McLane had inherited 12 years earlier. Under McLane, the line had not only been extended to Cumberland, but much of the physical plant of the original B&O had been rebuilt with the superior track materials.

As one of his first duties, President Swann began working to obtain the capital that would allow B&O to fulfill its charter. Through his efforts the railroad was able to take bids in 1849 to continue work west of Cumberland. Railroad building methods had advanced dramatically since B&O's early days, but the railroad would face challenges unlike any it had encountered before.

Construction west of Cumberland began in 1850 and would take almost three years to complete. The new trackage pushed southwest along the Potomac River to Piedmont Station where the line left the valley. The summit of the Alleghenies was reached at Altamont, Maryland, and B&O crossed the state line at Corinth, Virginia. Construction continued westward to Grafton, Virginia, then turned northwest toward Fairmont where it crossed the Monongahela River.

B&O finally reached the Ohio River at Wheeling, 379 miles west of Baltimore, in

B&O rails reached Martinsburg, Virginia (West Virginia after 1863) in 1842. Being about mid-way between Baltimore and Cumberland, Martinsburg was an ideal place for a division point. By 1849, a depot, roundhouse, shops, and other facilities were completed, and Martinsburg became a bustling railroad town. In July 1971, two Electro-Motive diesels idle at the facility next to the ancient roundhouse and shops. *William Myers*

December 1852. The work required 11 tunnels, over 100 bridges, and covered 200 track-miles. The total cost of the new line from Cumberland to Wheeling was $5.1 million. It had taken more than 24 years for the B&O to achieve the goal of its charter and cost three times as much as had originally been estimated (the project was budgeted for $5 million in 1827 but the final price tag in 1853 was $15 million). The Baltimore & Ohio having been completed to Wheeling, Thomas Swann resigned his post in April 1853.

B&O'S WESTERN FRONTIER

The Baltimore & Ohio was now exchanging freight and passenger traffic with the National Road and steamboats on the Ohio River, but sometimes the river was impassable at Wheeling, and B&O began contemplating a better river port farther downstream. At the same time B&O was building westward from Cumberland, a new line, the Northwestern Virginia Railroad, had been chartered in Virginia on February 14, 1851.

The NV would connect with B&O at

Grafton, about 100 miles west of Cumberland, and work on the line began in late 1852. Although it was supposedly a separate entity, the NV received much of its funding from the B&O. It was leased to the B&O in December 1856 and and it opened between Grafton and Parkersburg on May 1, 1857. In effect, the NV became B&O's third branch, and Parkersburg became its second port on the Ohio.

When B&O first reached the Ohio River in 1852, other railroads were being proposed or built in Ohio, Indiana, and Illinois. Critical to

B&O's expansion was the Central Ohio Railroad, chartered in February 1847 to build a rail line from Columbus to Bellaire, across the Ohio River from Wheeling. Construction began in 1852 and two years later the CO was finished. Several railroads had been built in the Buckeye State during the 1830s and 1840s to the so-called "Ohio gauge" of 4 feet, 10 inches, and the Central Ohio had adopted this slightly broad gauge.

Another Ohio railroad was being created in 1851 when two previously chartered lines, the Belpre & Cincinnati and the Franklin & Ohio, were consolidated to form the Marietta & Cincinnati. The M&C was established to connect the two Ohio River towns of Marietta and Cincinnati and thereby offer a means of transport that did not rely on the river. The line was built to standard gauge and opened in early 1857, about the same time Northwestern Virginia reached Parkersburg.

B&O connected with both the M&C and Central Ohio by river ferry. Transfer of cars to the M&C was relatively easy because the line was standard gauge. However, exchanging cars with Central Ohio was complicated by its difference in gauge with B&O—a problem overcome simply by using wider wheel treads.

John W. Garrett became B&O's seventh president on November 17, 1858. Garrett's reign would last until 1884 and would be exceeded in length by only one other president, Daniel Willard. By the time John Garrett had taken the presidency of B&O, the company had reached the Ohio River and was interchanging traffic with other railroads beyond. The rivalry between the cities of New York, Philadelphia, and Baltimore that had prompted the building of the Erie Canal, Pennsylvania's Main Line of Public Works, and the B&O continued, but the United States had become a much different nation since the late 1820s.

Thirty years after its conception, B&O was competing with other railroads, not canals. The New York Central and the Erie connected the Hudson River with Lake Erie. The Pennsylvania Railroad connected Philadelphia with the Ohio River at Pittsburgh. Across the former territorial lands that had become the states of Ohio, Indiana, and Illinois, many other railroads had been built to connect with these four trunk lines of the Northeast. These rail connections strengthened the commercial ties that had formed between the new states north of the Ohio River and Northeastern states.

Between Cumberland and Grafton the B&O had to build across four major mountain grades—all in West Virginia—to cross the Alleghenies. West from Cumberland the first was Seventeen-Mile Grade from Piedmont to Altamont; Cranberry Grade from Terra Alta to Rowlesburg was next, followed by Cheat River Grade from Rowlesburg to Tunnelton and Newburg Grade from Tunnelton to East Grafton. The eastbound train in this 1971 photo has just descended Cheat River Grade and now needs all the power it can muster to make it to the top of Cranberry Grade. The scene also shows M&K Junction tower and other facilities at Rowlesburg. *Jim O'Dell*

Construction west of Cumberland began in 1850, finally reaching the Ohio River at Wheeling in 1852. Grafton would become a major junction point and operations center for the B&O, as other lines were constructed out of Grafton to Parkersburg (another point on the Ohio River) and into the rich coal fields of the area. October 1970 finds three Electro-Motive F7As working eastward at Grafton yard. The imposing passenger depot and office building can be seen to the right. *Jim O'Dell*

As the Northern and Southern states became increasingly divided over social and political issues in the late 1850s, B&O had the misfortune of running directly through a region that would be in constant upheaval over the next few years. The election of Abraham Lincoln in 1860 as President of the United States prompted the secession of seven Southern states. The bombardment of Fort Sumter at Charleston in April 1861 started the war that would change America.

THE BATTLEFIELD RAILROAD

At the start of the Civil War, B&O served only two states directly, Maryland and Virginia. Maryland was a slave state and many of its citizens held pro-Southern sentiments, but it did not secede. On the other hand, Virginia seceded from the Union in 1861 although many the citizens of the territory through which the B&O operated in the western part of the state remained loyal to the union. This disparity would lead to creation of the West Virginia in 1863 with Wheeling as the first capital.

B&O was visited by violence a full year and a half before the war started on October 17, 1859, when the abolitionist John Brown and his band raided the federal arsenal at Harpers Ferry. An eastbound passenger train received gunfire and a baggage handler was seriously wounded, but the train was allowed to continue. The marauders were soon taken into custody by federal troops, but the incident was to be the first of many interruptions that B&O would suffer during the war.

After Lincoln's election, the seven states of the deep South seceded and the war officially began with the siege of Fort Sumter at Charleston. By the spring of 1861, militias were being mobilized, and four more states, including Virginia, seceded. The B&O had been conducting its business more or less as usual, but in mid-April Confederate troops took control of the area around Harpers Ferry. Trains were allowed to continue running, but under many restrictions.

After the first battle was fought at Big Bethel on June 10, the Confederates realized the value of B&O to the Union war effort, and a few days later, forces under the command of General T. J. "Stonewall" Jackson began to destroy the railroad. The Harpers Ferry bridge was blown up, and locomotives, rolling stock, and buildings at Martinsburg were burned.

The tide of the conflict would sweep across the operating territory of B&O for the next four years. Were it not for the dedication and ability of the railroad's management and employees to rise to the demands placed upon them during these times, the B&O could not have played its defining role during the hostilities. Dozens of miles of track and many bridges were demolished and rebuilt, some more than once. Although much of the B&O was out of service during a large part of the war, the Washington branch was very busy. As the only rail line to the nation's capital, it played a vital role moving troops and supplies to Southern battlefields.

One of B&O's biggest single contributions to the Union cause was its part in transporting 23,000 federal troops from northern Virginia to northwest Alabama in late September 1863. Following the Confederate victory at Chickamauga in mid-September, federal troops under General William Rosecrans came under siege at Chattanooga, and a relief force was dispatched from Washington. A troop move-

ment this size had never before been undertaken, and it required the coordination of several railroads.

Beginning on September 28, the Eleventh and Twelfth Corps of the Army of the Potomac traveled over the B&O from Washington to Wheeling, then over the Central Ohio to Columbus. The troops continued to Indianapolis, Louisville, and Nashville, detraining at Bridgeport, Alabama. From there, the Union army marched on to Chattanooga where they ended the siege of Rosecrans' army.

After the battle of Gettysburg in July 1863, the Confederate cause deteriorated, but Confederate raiders again attacked the B&O in July and October 1864. These would be the final military actions suffered by the B&O, and the war would end the following year with Robert E. Lee's surrender at Appomattox Court House on April 9.

With the conflict finally over, the United States once again looked toward westward expansion. The Baltimore & Ohio was likewise looking westward.

During the Civil War, B&O's Washington branch played a strategic role in the war effort. This view shows B&O's attractive Washington depot just after the Civil War, circa 1870, when dirt streets were still the norm. Except for the Capitol Building, the area has vastly changed since then. B&O Railroad Museum, courtesy Herbert H. Harwood Jr.

One of B&O's most-important accomplishments during the last half of the nineteenth century was the completion of its main line between Cumberland and Pittsburgh in 1871. The route required another crossing of the Alleghenies, this one via Sand Patch Grade in southwestern Pennsylvania. Helpers were regularly added to heavy westbound trains at Hyndman, 20 miles to the east of Sand Patch, the summit of the grade. In December 1967 two Electro-Motive diesels serving as a helper locomotive set glide past the summit marker at Sand Patch on their way back down the hill to help another train over the mountain. *Jim Boyd*

Baltimore Reaches Ohio–and Points West

CLOSING OUT THE NINETEENTH CENTURY

When the Civil War ended, America began to repair the destruction wrought by the struggle and again looked toward more western expansion. Ohio, Indiana, and Illinois—all of which were frontier states when the B&O was chartered in 1828—were now prosperous and well populated. During the final third of the 1800s, the U.S. would experience an era of unprecedented economic and industrial expansion.

The growth of commerce and industry had come about because of the ability of railroads to move great numbers of people and large quantities of freight over long distances quickly and economically. New railroads were under construction everywhere, and established systems were extending their lines into new territories. Baltimore & Ohio, the Pennsylvania, the New York Central, and the Erie had each served their own respective seaports (Baltimore, Philadelphia, New York, and Jersey City) before the war. As these four trunk lines built westward to reach new Midwestern cities, the Eastern seaport cities lost some of the influence over the railroads they had helped to create. The railroads searched for new business and were not above encroaching on the home turf of a competitor.

The formidable Pennsylvania Railroad, under the leadership of John Edgar Thomson, was acquiring other railroads and building new lines in B&O's backyard, making it B&O's chief competitor. B&O President John W. Garrett tried to counter this threat by reaching new markets and developing new traffic sources. Unfortunately, the PRR (and to a lesser degree, the NYC) always seemed to reach these new markets ahead of the B&O.

There were many other problems facing the entire railroad industry during this period. Ruthless competition between various lines resulted in rate wars that hurt the profit margins of the railroads involved. The Panic of 1873 was followed by a lengthy depression that further eroded railroad revenues. In 1877, several railroads cut wages in an effort to reduce operating expenses. This led to brief but bloody labor riots that began on the B&O and spread to other railroads during the summer. In spite of these difficulties, Garrett managed to triple B&O's mileage and increase the company's revenues almost threefold during his watch.

THE ROAD TO CHICAGO

As early as 1854, B&O had established connecting service with another railroad beyond its western terminus of Wheeling by means of a car ferry operating between Wheeling and the downstream town of Bellaire, Ohio. There, connection was made with the Central Ohio Railroad to Columbus (see previous chapter).

The financially frail CO struggled through the 1850s and the Civil War years until the B&O leased it on November 21, 1866. To improve its connection with what was now its Central Ohio Division, the B&O built a massive bridge across the Ohio River between Benwood, West Virginia, and Bellaire. Construction began in May 1868, and the structure went into service in June 1871. At the same time, Central Ohio's slightly broad gauge of 4 feet, 10 inches was changed to standard gauge.

Between 1848 and 1851, the Sandusky, Newark & Mansfield Railroad had been built northward from the Central Ohio at Newark to the Lake Erie port of Sandusky, Ohio. The

SN&M had been laid to a unique gauge of 5 feet, 4 inches but the route was soon realigned to Ohio's 4-foot 10-inch gauge. Commerce on Lake Erie grew during the 1860s, and Sandusky was one of several evolving port cities along the southern shore of the lake. The town was the northern terminus of Ohio's first railroad, the Mad River & Lake Erie. John Garrett saw access to Lake Erie as an important source of new traffic for the B&O and thus had subsidiary CO lease the SN&M in February 1869, giving B&O a gateway to the Great Lakes. The irony of the SN&M alliance is that it did indeed provide the B&O with a thriving port city on the Great Lakes—but in the long run it wasn't Sandusky. Renamed B&O's Lake Erie Division, the old SN&M became a vital link in B&O's earliest main line to Chicago—the ultimate Great Lakes port.

Chicago had become a prominent center of trade and manufacturing by the late 1860s. It was also becoming the busiest interchange point on America's burgeoning railway network, where major Northeastern trunk lines met the Western rail empires. The PRR had a through line to Chicago since 1858 through the Pittsburgh, Ft. Wayne & Chicago.

The B&O began surveying its own line to Chicago (under the title Baltimore, Pittsburgh & Chicago) in 1871. The first segment of the 260-mile extension was completed between Chicago Junction, about 90 miles north of Newark on the Lake Erie Division, and Deshler, Ohio, in 1873. The remainder of the line to Chicago was in place by 1875 and became B&O's Chicago Division.

When the B&O first reached Chicago, its passenger trains used Illinois Central tracks to enter downtown. The first B&O passenger station in Chicago was part of the Exposition Hall at Adams Street—approximately on the site of today's Art Institute at Adams and Michigan

Chicago Junction, Ohio, was just any old town on the Sandusky, Newark & Mansfield Railroad when the line was built from central Ohio to the shore of Lake Erie at Sandusky between 1848 and 1851. Then, in 1871, the B&O began surveying a line west to Chicago and completed the first segment west from Chicago Junction in 1873. Chicago Junction soon became a major railroad town, containing one of the B&O's major classification yards, a large depot, and division offices. The town was eventually renamed Willard in honor of one of B&O's presidents. *David P. Oroszi collection*

Avenue—near the shore of Lake Michigan, which at that time was at where Grant Park is today. In 1883, B&O began using a small brick station at the foot of Monroe Street (also near today's Art Institute). B&O moved to its third and final Chicago terminal, Grand Central Station, in 1891. Grand Central opened at Harrison and Wells in December 1890 and

was also home to the trains of Chicago Great Western and Wisconsin Central (later part of Soo Line).

B&O had its own track to Chicago, but as with St. Louis and other cities, the PRR and NYC had both arrived there years earlier. As an added disadvantage, B&O's route between Baltimore/Washington and Chicago was anything but direct. Although the Chicago Division was officially the Baltimore, Pittsburgh & Chicago, only the first and last cities in its name were on the route. It would be 1891 before the B&O would pass through Pittsburgh on its way to Chicago.

BALTIMORE & OHIO REACHES THE STEEL CITY

In the 1840s, prior to Thomas Swann's election as president of B&O, the railroad was debating which route the main line would follow west from Cumberland to reach the Ohio River. Three routes were proposed: one to Wheeling, one to

PUBLISHED SEMI-MONTHLY.

Pennsylvania, New York, and at all Ticket Offices of the B. & O. R. R.

Distributed in Maryland, Virginia, West Virginia, Ohio, Illinois,

BALTIMORE AND OHIO R.R.

TIME TABLES.

JUNE 1st, 1879.

Containing Time Tables of the Main Line Baltimore & O. R. R., and all Branches East and West of the Ohio River.

H. A. MILLER AND E. R. JONES................PUBLISHERS.

Three Fast Trains to the West Daily.

Quick Time! Elegant Equipment! Steel Rails! Fine Scenery! Splendid Hotels!

TICKET OFFICES.

BALTIMORE.
149 Baltimore Street, South-east Corner of Calvert, 99 Thames Street, and Camden Station.

WASHINGTON.
603, 619 and 1435 Pennsylvania Av., and at Depot, Corner New Jersey Avenue and C Street.

L. M. COLE, Gen. Ticket Agent.

WM. M. CLEMENTS, Master of Transportation.

A B&O timetable from 1879 advertised "Three Fast Trains to the West." At that time, places like Chicago, St. Louis, and Ohio points were considered the "West" and not Midwest as they are today. *Collection of David P. Oroszi*

For nearly 80 years B&O trains called at the Solon Beman-designed Grand Central Station in Chicago. The terminal was completed in 1890 and first served trains of Wisconsin Central. B&O moved its trains to Grand Central in 1891, leased the station in 1900, and later purchased it. Grand Central was considered more architecturally significant than most of the other rail terminals in the city. It was razed in 1971 to make way for a considerably less aesthetic, non-railroad building. *Collection of Mike Schafer*

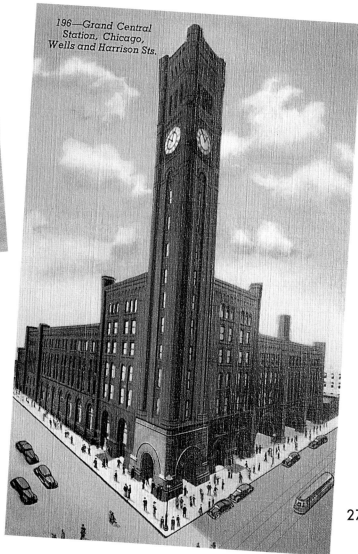

196—Grand Central Station, Chicago, Wells and Harrison Sts.

In 1868 B&O took control of the Pittsburgh & Connellsville Railroad, which paved the way for B&O's entry into Pittsburgh from the east. Two more routes into Pittsburgh would eventually materialize for the B&O, one from Wheeling, West Virginia, and one from Akron, Ohio. The base of operations for the Pittsburgh area would be Glenwood Yard on the southeast side of Pittsburgh. On April 1, 1983, GP38 3831 takes an eastbound freight past WJ Tower at the east end of Glenwood. *Steve Salamon*

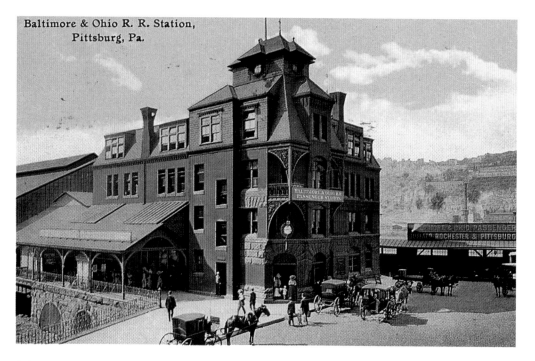

Baltimore & Ohio R. R. Station, Pittsburg, Pa.

B&O's main passenger facility in downtown Pittsburgh was located on the south side of the business district parallel to the nearby Monongahela River. Because it was a stub-end depot (no through tracks), through trains had to make a reverse move in one direction to reach the station. This cumbersome arrangement was eliminated when B&O's through passenger trains were moved across the river to the Pittsburgh & Lake Erie in 1915. Commuter trains remained at the downtown depot into the 1980s. *Collection of Mike Schafer*

Parkersburg, and the third to Pittsburgh. In response, the Pennsylvania legislature approved two railroad bills in 1846. One bill allowed B&O to build between Cumberland and Pittsburgh while the other sanctioned the construction of a different railroad between Harrisburg—the state capital—and Pittsburgh. The B&O bill did not take effect until July 1847, and by that time the Pennsylvania Railroad was building its main line westward from Harrisburg. The State of Pennsylvania cancelled the legislation that permitted the B&O to reach Pittsburgh, which led B&O to choose the route to Wheeling. It marked a victory for the PRR but also typified the emerging rivalry between B&O and PRR.

In its next attempt to reach Pittsburgh, the B&O underwrote the construction of the Pittsburgh & Connellsville Railroad. The P&C had been completed between its namesake cities at the start of the Civil War, but the PRR had persuaded the Pennsylvania legislature to enact legislation that allowed the Pennsy to take over the P&C in 1864. B&O President Garrett took the issue to court, and the Pennsylvania Supreme Court eventually decided in B&O's favor in 1868. P&C was returned to B&O control, and the line was renamed Pittsburgh, Washington & Baltimore. Construction from Connellsville, Pennsylvania, toward Cumberland resumed and the 150-mile line was finished in May 1871. The completion of B&O's branch to Pittsburgh, with its growing iron and steel industry, gave the road a new market for coal coming from mines along its main line in West Virginia.

Also in 1871, Garrett was piecing together a second entry to Pittsburgh, this one from the west. In that year, B&O took control of Hempfield Railroad between Wheeling and Washington, Pennsylvania, and the line was renamed Wheeling, Pittsburgh & Baltimore Railroad. A dozen years later, B&O closed the gap between Washington and Pittsburgh by acquiring a narrow-gauge line, the Pittsburgh Southern Railroad. The PS was rebuilt to standard gauge, and a bridge across the Monongahela River near Pittsburgh connected the PS with the Pittsburgh & Connellsville. In 1885, the Pittsburgh Southern was renamed Baltimore & Ohio Short Line; B&OSL was merged into Wheeling, Pittsburgh & Baltimore in 1887.

BEYOND PITTSBURGH

Through service to Chicago had been established by B&O in 1874, but the course it followed from Baltimore to the Midwestern metropolis via Wheeling and Newark, Ohio, was a distant third to those taken by PRR and NYC. Garrett needed a more direct route to Chicago. PRR and NYC's subsidiary Pittsburgh & Lake Erie eclipsed B&O's presence in the Steel City, so B&O had to work hard for its share of traffic from Pittsburgh.

B&O gained its third line into Pittsburgh when it bought controlling interest in Pittsburgh & Western 1884. Initially narrow gauge, the P&W ran northward from the town of Allegheny, across the Allegheny River from Pittsburgh, to Youngstown, Ohio, where it split for Akron and Fairport, Ohio—the latter on Lake Erie. With the addition of P&W, which had been converted to standard gauge before B&O takeover, the B&O gained a northern route from Pittsburgh. To link the P&W with its other lines in the city—the Pittsburgh & Connellsville and Wheeling, Pittsburgh & Baltimore—the B&O acquired the Pittsburgh Junction Railroad, a 4.4-mile-long connecting line that was built during 1883–84.

During 1890–91, B&O constructed a new 73-mile line between Akron and Chicago Junction, the Akron & Chicago Junction Railroad. When the A&CJ was completed, it created a new mainline route between the East Coast and Chicago that passed through Pittsburgh. Freight traffic began moving over A&CJ in August 1891 and B&O's East Coast–Chicago passenger service began operating via Pittsburgh in May 1893.

As the A&CJ was being built, B&O was also in the process of acquiring a route to Cleveland. By the 1880s, Cleveland had become a prominent port on Lake Erie and a center of commerce and manufacturing. B&O gained access to the city when it purchased a shortline that crossed A&CJ at Akron. Incorporated in 1871, the Valley Railway Company's 75-mile route followed the Cuyahoga River southward from Cleveland to Akron. It continued through Canton to reach its southern terminus at Valley Junction. The VR was completed in 1882, and B&O gained control of the road in 1890, making Cleveland its third (after Sandusky and Fairport) and most important Lake Erie port. B&O served many customers along the Cuyahoga River in Cleveland, and the terminal facilities were consolidated with Valley Railway in 1895 to form the Cleveland Terminal & Valley Railroad. The CT&V was operated separately until it became part of B&O in 1915.

BALTIMORE & OHIO SOUTHWESTERN

A few years after the B&O had reached the Ohio River at Wheeling, a second line, the Northwestern Virginia Railroad, was opened to Parkersburg in 1857. Although the NV was in need of much improvement when it was leased to B&O in 1856, the line provided an important connection to a southern Ohio railroad across the river, the Marietta & Cincinnati Railroad. Built to standard gauge, the M&C connected with the B&O by way of a nine-mile ferry trip down the Ohio River from Marietta to Parkersburg.

As B&O resumed expanding its system following the Civil War, it built two bridges across the Ohio River, one at Wheeling and the other at Parkersburg. The bridge at Parkersburg crossed the river to reach M&C at Belpre, Ohio, a few miles southwest of Marietta. Work on the 7,100-foot structure (including approaches) started in July 1869, and the bridge opened on January 7, 1871.

The Marietta & Cincinnati had been funded in part by the towns of Marietta, Chillicothe, and Cincinnati, as well as the southern Ohio counties of Washington, Athens, and Ross. The road built its line across southern Ohio to connect with Little Miami Railroad at Loveland, about 20 miles from Cincinnati. M&C trains used the tracks of Little Miami from Loveland to the Little Miami depot at Cincinnati.

The M&C completed its own line around the north side of the city in 1861 to connect with the Cincinnati, Hamilton & Dayton Railroad at Ludlow Grove (later named Spring Grove), and trackage rights brought M&C trains to the CH&D's Cincinnati depot. In 1865, the M&C began using the Plum Street Station, recently completed by the Indianapolis, Cincinnati & Lafayette Railroad. A new six-mile connecting line was completed between Ludlow Grove and downtown Cincinnati in 1872, providing M&C with its own route into the inner city.

Although the B&O provided the M&C with a sizeable amount of overhead traffic to and from Cincinnati, on-line traffic failed to develop to sufficient levels, and the M&C was in destitution through the 1870s. In 1882 B&O took control of the M&C and reorganized the line as Cincinnati, Washington & Baltimore Railway. In 1889 the line from Belpre to Cincinnati was renamed as the Baltimore & Ohio Southwestern Railroad.

At Cincinnati, another line reached westward to St. Louis. Built to six-foot gauge, the Ohio & Mississippi Railroad was completed between Cincinnati and East St. Louis, Illinois, in 1857. Soon, B&O, the M&C, and the O&M offered an all-rail passage from Baltimore to St. Louis that was billed at the time as the "American Central Route."

This route was an improvement over riverboats because it did not cease operations during the winter months, but there were problems with the connection at Cincinnati. The fact that the M&C was standard gauge and O&M was broad gauge meant there was no physical connection between the two lines, requiring the transfer of passengers and freight on horse-drawn wagons through the streets of Cincinnati.

Like the M&C, the six-foot-gauge Ohio & Mississippi was also struggling financially. The railroad was plagued with heavy debt and expenses while producing inadequate revenues. The line traversed southern Indiana and Illinois, areas that were (and still are) sparsely populated and then still underdeveloped. In addition to its Cincinnati–East St. Louis main line, the O&M fielded two branches. One headed south from the main line at North Vernon, Indiana, to Jeffersonville, Indiana, across the Ohio River from Louisville, Kentucky. The other branch ran diagonally across Illinois from Beardstown on the Illinois River to Shawneetown on the Ohio River, crossing O&M's main line at Flora.

O&M converted its track to standard gauge on July 13, 1871, but the road's financial condition caused the B&O to keep its distance for several years more. Not until 1893 was the O&M acquired to complete B&O's route to St. Louis. The O&M was formally merged into Baltimore & Ohio Southwestern in 1900.

Meanwhile, the Columbus & Cincinnati Midland Railroad had built a 70-mile line southwest from Columbus to meet M&C at Midland City, Ohio. Completed in 1885, the C&CM would become part of the B&O map five years later and provide B&O with a direct through route between Pittsburgh and Cincinnati via Wheeling and Columbus.

NEW TRACK IN MARYLAND AND VIRGINIA

A new line to carry traffic westward from Washington directly to the main line at Point of Rocks was one of the first additions B&O made after the war. Construction on the Metropolitan Branch began in 1866.

The ideal course for the new branch would

In 1882 B&O took direct control over the Marietta & Cincinnati, which had built its line across southern Ohio between the namesake cities. At Greenfield, Ohio, the former M&C line crossed Paint Creek on a sizeable trestle. The original structure was replaced by the bridge in this picture, which was taken on March 10, 1985, as train WLTT (Washington–Louisville Trailer Train) headed east towards Wilmington, Delaware. *Brad McClelland*

have been along the Potomac River, but the C&O Canal had already taken that route. The Metropolitan Branch instead was located north of the river and crossed hilly terrain, requiring many fills, cuts, and bridges. The 43-mile project took seven years and $3.5 million to complete. Service on the Metropolitan Branch began on May 25, 1873, and most through passenger and mail traffic between Baltimore and points west was then rerouted through Washington. The original main line via Ellicotts Mills was retained primarily for coal and freight traffic.

With a main line now running through the nation's capital, B&O proclaimed itself "The Capitol Route." The image of the U.S. Capitol building's dome became the company trademark on everything B&O, from timetables and promotional brochures to locomotives.

Many improvements were also being made in the Baltimore terminal area. B&O had outgrown its first Baltimore station at Pratt Street by the early 1850s, so a new depot was built at Camden Street. Camden Station was opened in 1857, and it served as B&O's main passenger facility in Baltimore for 40 years. It also housed

the railroad's headquarters until 1882 when the offices were moved to a new seven-story office building in downtown Baltimore.

In 1848–49, the B&O built a branch to Locust Point where freight yards and docks were built to transfer coal for export to ships calling at Baltimore's harbor. During the next 20 years, grain elevators and warehouses were built dockside to handle increasing shipments of grain and general merchandise. To relieve some of the congestion at Locust Point, a new coal dock was built in the 1880s at Curtis Bay.

Seeking to expand into Southern markets, B&O began leasing a series of shortlines in western Virginia. The Winchester & Potomac, whose 22-mile line northeast from Winchester, Virginia, connected with the B&O at Harpers Ferry, was leased on July 1, 1867. Shortly after its completion in 1870, the 19-mile Winchester & Strasburg Railroad—connecting its namesake cities—was also leased. In 1874 a third company, the Virginia Midland Railroad, had completed its line southward from Strasburg to Harrisonburg, 50 miles. The VM had come under B&O control in September 1873.

A fourth company in this series, the Valley

Cincinnati, Hamilton & Dayton 4-4-0 No. 123 is northbound with a passenger train at the first Dayton Union Station in 1896. This station was used by predecessor railroads to the B&O, PRR, NYC, and Erie. The second Union Station, which stood just to the north of the one pictured here, was opened in 1900. *Collection of David P. Oroszi*

B&O reached the St. Louis gateway via the Ohio & Mississippi Railroad, which was completed between Cincinnati and East St Louis, Illinois, in 1857. B&O acquired the O&M in 1893 and merged it into the Baltimore & Ohio Southwestern in 1900. January 3, 1971, finds the eastbound C&O/B&O *George Washington* leaving St. Louis via the Eads Bridge over the Mississippi River. *D. A. Woodworth Jr.*

Railroad, had been chartered in February 1866. The VRR was to build a line from Harrisonburg to Salem, but construction proceeded very slowly. The line had only reached Lexington by 1883 and by that time President Garrett was preoccupied with extending B&O westward. The curtailed venture into the deep South would remain as only a branch from the main line at Harpers Ferry and would also be B&O's only trackage in the state of Virginia.

THE ROYAL BLUE LINE

During the 1870s, B&O had been operating its trains to Philadelphia over the rails of Philadelphia, Wilmington & Baltimore Railroad. Beyond Philadelphia, B&O used trackage rights over the PRR to reach Jersey City, across the harbor from New York City. At the same time, Edgar Thomson was expanding the PRR into new territory on the eastern end of its system, intensifying the rivalry with B&O.

Thomson's PRR had already invaded B&O domain in the late 1860s when it acquired the dormant charter to the Baltimore & Potomac Railroad. With PRR backing, the B&P built a line between Washington and Baltimore in the early 1870s. PRR had already reach Baltimore from Harrisburg though subsidiary Northern Central. PRR had reached Washington and broken B&O's monopoly on the capital.

PRR then staged another coup in 1881 by outbidding B&O for control of PW&B. Garrett had attempted to purchase control of the PW&B, but the Pennsy raised the bid price for shares of PW&B stock. Although the PRR took charge of PW&B, B&O trains were allowed to use the line to Philadelphia until the traffic agreements to handle through business were cancelled in 1884.

By that time, Garrett had obtained the charter of Delaware Western to build his own line between Baltimore and Philadelphia. He secured passage for B&O trains east of Philadelphia over the Philadelphia & Reading Railroad to Bound Brook, New Jersey. From Bound Brook, B&O trains continued on the Central Railroad of New Jersey (Jersey Central) to reach the CNJ terminal at Jersey City. Passengers could then take a ferry across New York harbor to reach downtown Manhattan.

Paralleling the PW&B, B&O's new route to Philadelphia opened in September 1886. It was an expensive line to build, with several large bridges, the largest spanning the Susquehanna River at Havre de Grace, Maryland. The 111-mile route would soon be named the Royal Blue Line for the premier passenger trains that the B&O would inaugurate between Jersey City and Washington.

B&O managed to establish its own freight terminal in lower New York Harbor when it bought controlling interest in the Staten Island Rapid Transit Railway in 1885. Staten Island was one of New York City's five boroughs (after 1898) and the only one west of the Hudson River. To reach Staten Island and the SIRT, B&O built its own line from the CNJ at Cranford Junction and constructed a swing bridge across Arthur Kill, the river that separated Staten Island from New Jersey. From the SIRT yard at St. George, B&O traffic was floated across New York harbor—an operation that required a flotilla of tugboats, carfloats, and barges.

When the B&O bought the SIRT it also inherited a 22-mile commuter operation, between St. George (where connection was made with the Staten Island Ferry from Manhattan) and Tottenville, across Arthur Kill from

Camden Station, B. & O. Railroad, Camden & Howard streets, Baltimore, Md.

Camden Station was opened for service in 1857 and served as B&O's main Baltimore passenger facility for through trains for 40 years. It also housed the railroad's headquarters until 1882, when the offices were moved to a new seven-story office building in downtown Baltimore. *Collection of David P. Oroszi*

Perth Amboy, New Jersey. The commuter line was electrified in 1925; it was B&O's second and last electrification project.

BALTIMORE BELT RAILROAD

Although B&O could now offer its own service between Washington and New York, there was a gap in the rail line at Baltimore. The Philadelphia extension's terminal was at Canton, on the north shore of Baltimore Harbor, and B&O had no connecting trackage to the Washington and Cumberland main lines; traffic operating to and from Philadelphia had to be transferred by car ferry across Baltimore Harbor from the B&O docks at Locust Point. It was a cumbersome and time-consuming arrangement that had to be rectified if B&O were to effectively compete with the PRR in the Washington–New York corridor.

B&O established the Baltimore Belt Railroad in the late 1880s to build a connecting line. In the 70 years since the founding of the B&O, Baltimore had grown into a large city, and property values were high. The Belt Line would be one of the railroad's costliest additions. An

elevated line was first suggested, but local opposition killed that proposal. Instead, B&O routed the tracks northward from Camden Station *under* the city through a 7300-foot tunnel to be dug beneath Howard Street. Eastbound trains would climb a constant 0.8 percent grade through the tunnel. The B&O would also build a new station at Mount Royal, located at the north end of the tunnel. Construction of the 7.2-mile Belt Line began in September 1890 while work on the tunnel itself began the following year.

The use of steam locomotives in such a long tunnel would create ventilation problems, and city ordinances would have required the railroad to build tall smokestacks to dissipate smoke and fumes vented from the tunnel. To solve the predicament, the railroad turned to a new form of traction. Electric locomotives would be used to pull entire trains, steam engines and all, beneath the city. The Howard Street Tunnel would be the world's first mainline electrification of a steam railroad.

The application of electric traction to trunk-line railroad operations had never been attempted, but B&O's directors decided to take the gamble. The railroad hired the General Electric Company in 1892 to carry out the work, even though GE's experience was limited to only a few small mining locomotives.

The Belt Line was completed in early 1895, but electrification work was still under way. The first trains that used the Howard Street tunnel on May 1, 1895, were pulled by coke-fired steam locomotives which produced much less smoke. The power distribution system was finished and the first electric locomotive hauled a test train on June 27. B&O introduced the public to electric traction on July 1 when electric locomotive No. 1 pulled a special train carrying dignitaries through the tunnel. Within a year, three electric locomotives were in regular service moving trains under the streets of Baltimore. The electrics only worked eastbound trains since the steam locomotives on westbound trains could drift downgrade through the tunnel.

Mount Royal Station opened in September 1896, giving the B&O a second terminal in its hometown. The Baltimore Belt Railroad with its revolutionary motive power was a success. Together with the Philadelphia extension, it had allowed B&O to compete with PRR for Philadelphia–Washington traffic. But both lines were very costly to build and the debt strained the railroad's fiscal health.

continued on page 38

GLIDING MOTION!

Its lower center of gravity, rubber-cushioned, roller bearing trucks and stabilizers give a *balanced* ride —so restful and smooth, it's like *gliding* through the air! Indeed, you are on your way before you feel the train move. An ocean liner couldn't leave its dock more gracefully!

The entire atmosphere of the train is one of refinement and comfort. Kept clean and comfortable by B & O's improved type of air-conditioning that controls temperature and humidity the year 'round, regardless of the weather.

BALTIMORE AND OHIO

IN STREAMLINED TRAINS ◆

It was only appropriate that the showcase train of B&O's "Royal Blue" route to Jersey City be named the Royal Blue. Launched in 1935, the Royal Blue became B&Os first train to be streamlined, in 1937. This train folder explained the features of the newly streamlined train, which initially was powered by steam. Alas, the Royal Blue Line and nearly all its passenger trains fell victim to the powerful and parallel Pennsylvania Railroad, and B&O passenger service east of Baltimore was discontinued in 1958. *William F. Howes, Jr. collection*

Originally B&O gained access to Jersey City via trackage rights on rival Pennsylvania Railroad east of Philadelphia. However, in 1884 B&O acquired trackage rights over the more friendly Philadelphia & Reading Railroad between Philadelphia and Bound Brook, New Jersey, and thence over the Central Railroad of New Jersey (Jersey Central) between Bound Brook and CNJ's Jersey City Terminal. Passengers could then take ferries or B&O busses (themselves transported on the ferries) across New York Harbor to reach downtown Manhattan. In 1954 the *Marylander* leaves CNJ Terminal for Washington. *Herbert H. Harwood Jr.*

36

B&O managed to establish its own freight terminal in lower New York Harbor when it acquired controlling interest in the Staten Island Rapid Transit Railway in 1885. From the SIRT yard at St. George, New York, on Staten Island, B&O traffic was floated across New Your Harbor to Jersey City, requiring a flotilla of tug-boats, carfloats, and barges. This tug and carfloat are at St. George in 1954. *I. Cusik, collection of Herbert H. Harwood Jr.*

The Baltimore Belt Railroad was established in the late 1880s to build a line around Baltimore to link the new Philadelphia extension with the original main line west out of Camden Station. North from Camden Station a 7,300-foot tunnel was burrowed under Howard Street, with a new station at the north end of the tunnel at Mount Royal (page 39). Electric locomotives were developed by the General Electric Company for use in the tunnel—one of the first applications of electric locomotives for mainline railroads in the U.S. This photo shows the south portal of the Howard Street Tunnel, the entrance to the lower level of Camden Station, and an electric locomotive. *Collection of William F. Howes Jr.*

Continued from page 35

THE POST-GARRETT B&O

From 1858, when he was elected president of B&O, until his death in 1884, John W. Garrett transformed America's first common-carrier railroad into a 1,700-mile system that stretched from Baltimore to Lake Erie and Chicago. Under his management, Garrett shaped the B&O that would endure another century in spite of the railroad's financial hardships and operating handicaps.

Shortly before his death, Garrett relinquished his presidency to his son Robert, but the younger Garrett's term would last less than three years. Robert Garrett supervised the completion of the Philadelphia extension that his father had started, but health problems prompted him to resign in 1887.

The board of directors then elected Robert Garrett's first vice president, Samuel Spencer, to the presidency on December 10, 1887. Spencer would occupy the office for only a year, but he brought with him a great deal of practical experience and the some good financial connections. He undertook reforms of the company's accounting and bookkeeping practices, and his policies reduced B&O's floating debt by $5 million.

While seeking new cash from New York banks, Spencer was also looking for ways to cut costs. He sold the railroad's telegraph system to Western Union and its fleet of sleeping cars to the Pullman Palace Car Company, which then operated them on B&O trains under contract. In spite of his achievements, Spencer found a lack of support for his reforms among board members. He resigned on December 19, 1888, and was replaced by Charles F. Mayer, B&O's tenth president.

Mayer's administration made several important additions to B&O that have been previously covered, notably the Pittsburgh & Western, the Baltimore Belt Railroad, and the Ohio & Mississippi. Several new lines were also added to the B&O map in Pennsylvania, West Virginia, and Ohio in the early 1890s.

In 1890, a positive development took place in B&O's boardroom. From its beginnings, the railroad had relied heavily on the City of Baltimore and the State of Maryland for financial support. As a result, B&O's board of directors traditionally had been comprised of twelve stockholder directors, seven directors representing Baltimore, and four directors representing Maryland.

At that time, the City of Baltimore sold off its B&O stock and withdrew its directors from the board. The State of Maryland also sold its shares of B&O preferred stock and reduced the number of its directors on the board from four to two. The number of members on the B&O's board dropped from 23 to 14, and the result of these changes was a shift away from the influence of Baltimore and Maryland in the direction of the railroad. The investment bankers that now sat on the board took a more prominent role in the management of the railroad. The interests that they represented were concerned with sound business practice rather than political obligations.

RECEIVERSHIP AND REORGANIZATION

The Philadelphia extension and Baltimore Belt Railroad were both very expensive projects for B&O, and the railroad had to carry an exceptionally heavy debt load. To make things worse, the company had been paying dividends of $8 to $10 per share from the mid-1860s through the late 1880s. Samuel

Spencer had put an end to the practice in 1888, but by that time B&O was already on its way to the poor farm.

The Panic of 1893 drew the nation into economic depression in the mid 1890s and business activity slowed. Traffic on the B&O dropped significantly. Charles Mayer gave his best effort to control expenses but revenues continued to fall (along with B&O's stock price) during the 1890s.

In the face of rising deficits, Charles Mayer resigned in December 1895 and was replaced by John K. Cowen in January 1896. Five weeks after Cowen became president, the B&O entered into receivership. Cowen and Oscar Murray, B&O's first vice president, were appointed receivers by the federal court in Baltimore. They immediately embarked on a reorganization plan to straighten out the railroad's finances and at the same time rebuild its physical plant. Ironically, Cowen and Murray undertook many of the same reforms that Samuel Spencer had tried to institute during his brief tenure in 1888.

When the company emerged from receivership two years later, it was not only financially stronger but many improvements had been made to the physical plant. Over 200 new locomotives and 28,000 new freight cars had been purchased, and more than 120,000 tons of new steel rails were laid as many miles of track were rebuilt.

As the nineteenth century drew to a close, B&O was entering an era of relative stability and prosperity. The railroad had grown to a 3,000-mile network that connected Philadelphia, Baltimore, and Washington with Chicago and St. Louis. Compared with its rival Northeastern carriers, B&O had more grades to climb, more curves to round, and more tunnels to pass through than even the PRR, a mountain railroad in its own right. Nonetheless, the future seemed to bode well for B&O at the beginning of the twentieth century.

Designed by E. Francis Baldwin and Josias Pennington, Mount Royal Station opened in 1896 as part of the construction of the Baltimore Belt Railroad. It was planted at the north end of the Howard Street Tunnel, which begins at Camden Station on the south side of downtown Baltimore and runs due north to Mount Royal Avenue. The tracks emerged right from the tunnel and into the train shed, which is partially visible behind the depot building in this scene from circa 1900. Because the tracks approach the depot through the tunnel, cuts, and street underpasses, the appearance is that of a railroad facility without a railroad. After the discontinuance of Royal Blue Line passenger service in 1958, the depot became home for the Maryland Institute. It still stands north of downtown Baltimore and is one of the few major passenger stations in North America to retain its traditional train shed. *Collection of William F. Howes Jr.*

Cleveland, Ohio, has always been a transportation hub and manufacturing center and an important location for the B&O. The railroad had two different lines into the city. The CT&V Subdivision came from the south via Akron, and the CL&W Subdivision from the west via Lester, Ohio. On August 16, 1984, Electro-Motive GP9 No. 6091 is taking a cut of cars to the Conrail interchange at Whiskey Island. Bridge 464 was one of three lift bridges between Whiskey Island and the B&O's main yard at Clark Avenue. *Dennis Nehrenz*

CHAPTER 3

Baltimore & Ohio in the New Century

1900-1945: FROM WILLARD TO WAR

A revitalized Baltimore & Ohio entered the twentieth century facing growing competition, not only from the Pennsylvania and other railroads, but from new contenders as well. During the 1800s, railroads had altered virtually every aspect of American life, from commerce and travel to the geographic character of the nation. The industrial development that railroads fostered made steel and other materials available at reasonable prices. The refining of petroleum created several new types of fuels while electrical engineering had moved out of the laboratory and into the home and workplace.

As all these elements came together, new sources of energy were appearing during the 1890s. Just as steam propulsion had made railroads practical in the 1830s, the development of the internal-combustion engine and electricity gave birth to new forms of transport. The electric interurban railroad was basically a progression of the streetcar that offered a fast and clean alternative to the soot and cinders of the existing "steam railroads." Interurbans spread quickly during the first ten years of the new century with most of them being built in Midwestern states. At first, some lines managed to steal a sizeable amount of short-haul passenger traffic from the steam roads, but many went out of business during the 1920s, as another new means of travel became popular.

Automobiles first appeared around the turn of the century as horseless carriages and were little more than toys for the wealthy. Their use was limited anyway since most roads of that period were unpaved and impassable in foul weather. Gradually, the reliability of the "flivver" rose and the price came down. As roads improved, automobiles became more popular with the public, and the railroads lost more passenger revenue.

A more serious threat to the railroads was also in its infancy during these years. The first motor trucks were little more than delivery wagons with a gasoline engine (or an electric motor and a ton of batteries) replacing a team of horses. As with the early automobiles, mechanical limitations and inferior roads kept most early trucking to within towns and cities. But with time, both trucks and roads advanced, and railroads would begin to lose freight shipments to motor carriers.

Nonetheless, the railroads were still the dominant form of transport at century's turn. Although at times they could be one another's most bitter enemy, they could also be close allies if it were in their own best interests. To stabilize railroad competition and rate-cutting, Pennsylvania Railroad president Alexander Cassatt negotiated an agreement with the New York Central by which the two roads would purchase stock in the smaller trunk lines of the East. What happened next caused many citizens of Baltimore to believe John Garrett would roll over in his grave.

THE PENNSY TAKES OVER

The Pennsylvania Railroad began buying B&O stock in 1899 and within a year held enough shares to seat two of its officers on the B&O board. Two more PRR men were brought into the boardroom in 1901, and Alexander Cassatt began to exercise his railroad's control of the B&O. John Cowen, who had masterfully guided the B&O through its period of receivership, was asked to resign the office of president. The PRR executives commended him for his service to the company and offered to him his previous position as general counsel, which he accepted. The board promptly replaced Cowen with a Pennsylvania officer. On June 1, 1901, Leonor F. Loree was elected as the B&O's twelfth president. Loree had been a vice president of the PRR's lines west of Pittsburgh and had almost 25 years of operating experience when he came to the B&O.

Although it seemed that the PRR's dominance could only bring misfortune to the B&O, Loree actually planned to make substantial upgrades to B&O's operations and physical plant. He began to implement what was to be a 20-year program of improvements. Freight yards were rebuilt, and many miles of the main line were relocated to enhance the movement of traffic. To increase train speeds over steep mountain grades, the B&O put the first articulated steam locomotive in the U.S. into service.

Although controlled by the Pennsylvania Railroad, the B&O began buying stock in the Philadelphia & Reading, which in turn controlled the Central Railroad Company of New Jersey (Jersey Central). Since the B&O had established traffic agreements with the two lines between Philadelphia and Jersey City, the B&O wanted to ensure that they remained friendly connections.

Meanwhile, a new passenger terminal was being planned for Washington. It was to be a joint facility shared with the PRR, and construction began in 1903. Washington Union Station opened in October 1907, replacing B&O's old depot at the corner of New Jersey Avenue and C Street (page 23).

During Loree's term, several new routes were acquired. One was the Ohio River Railroad, built in the 1880s southwesterly from Wheeling along the south bank of its namesake river to Parkersburg, Huntington, and Kenova, West Virginia. The predominant traffic on this line was oil and petroleum products. The B&O leased the ORRR in September 1901 and bought the road in 1912.

At that time, the B&O was also looking for a more direct route for coal destined from mines along its lines in West Virginia destined for Cleveland, a major manufacturing center and transportation hub. Iron ore shipped from Minnesota to this Lake Erie port and coal from southern Ohio and West Virginia made Cleveland an ideal site for steel production. The B&O had first reached the city in 1890 when it acquired the Valley Railway Company

between Cleveland and Valley Junction. With its procurement of the Cleveland, Lorain & Wheeling Railway at the turn of the century, the B&O gained a second route to Cleveland.

The origins of the CL&W dated from 1871 when the Elyria & Black River Railroad chartered an eight-mile line from Elyria to Charlestown (later Lorain) on Lake Erie. Shortly after the E&BR was completed, it was sold to the Lake Shore & Tuscarawas Valley Railway. The LS&TV built southward from Elyria to Urichsville (about 40 miles northwest of the river) before falling into receivership in 1874. The Cleveland, Tuscarawas Valley & Wheeling Railway bought the LS&TV and began building from Urichsville to the Ohio River. The line was finished in May 1880, creating a new route between the Ohio River and Lake Erie.

The CTV&W itself went into receivership a couple of years later. It was sold and reorganized by its new owners as the Cleveland, Lorain & Wheeling Railroad in 1883. A branch was built at the south end of the railroad to connect with the Central Ohio Railroad at Bellaire in 1887. At the north end of the line, a 30-mile branch from the main stem of the CL&W at Lester was opened to Cleveland in 1895.

When the B&O came out of its own receivership in 1899, it saw the CL&W as a good route from the coal fields to Cleveland and began purchasing CL&W stock. After gaining control of the CL&W, the B&O initiated a rebuilding program for the entire line that included a new yard at Holloway, Ohio and several segments of double track.

The mining of coal in southern Ohio began as early as 1800 and flourished for more than a century. The B&O entered the coal fields in southeastern Ohio in 1872 when the Newark, Somerset & Straitsville Railroad was leased to B&O subsidiary Sandusky, Mansfield & Newark. From its connection with the Central Ohio at Newark, the NS&S meandered southward about 45 miles. The Central Ohio controlled the SM&N, and both lines lost their identities when they were blended into the B&O corporate structure in 1915.

During his term, Loree increased the B&O's presence in the southeastern Ohio coal region. A railroad named the Ohio & Little Kanawha ran from Marietta up the Muskingum River to Zanesville. Since the O&LK connected with the B&O at each end, it was no surprise when the road became part of the B&O shortly after the turn of the century.

On January 1, 1904, Leonor Loree resigned

The new century would bring additional expansion to the B&O, two world wars, and dieselization. B&O bought controlling interest in the Buffalo, Rochester & Pittsburgh in 1929, giving B&O entry into western New York State. On a late summer's day in 1975, a Pittsburgh-bound freight awaiting a new train crew holds at B&O's stately depot at East Salamanca, New York, junction point of the Buffalo and Rochester branches of the former BR&P. *Mike Schafer*

his presidency of the B&O, exactly 31 months after the day he was elected. He went west to become president of the Chicago, Rock Island & Pacific Railway. There was no doubt that his reign had been of great benefit to the B&O in spite of the fact that he was placed on the throne by the B&O's antagonist, the Pennsylvania Railroad. Even after Loree's departure, work continued on the many improvements that he had started.

PHILADELPHIA RETREATS, BALTIMORE REBOUNDS

Public sentiment against business monopolies, or trusts, was running high, and few industries in America wielded such influence as the railroads. Congress and President Theodore Roosevelt responded by enacting legislation that gave the Interstate Commerce Commission more control over the nation's railroads. Although the ICC had been created in 1887, it was the Elkins Act of 1904 and the Hepburn Act of 1906 that gave the agency real authority to regulate the rail industry.

Faced with stricter government regulation, the PRR began to gradually sell off its B&O stock (PRR would, however, maintain its presence on the board of directors until 1912). The presidency returned to a B&O man when Oscar G. Murray assumed the post on the day Leonor Loree stepped down. Murray was a vice president under John Cowen and Loree and co-receiver with Cowen during the railroad's reorganization of 1896–98.

From 1900 to 1910, the B&O had grown from about 3,200 miles to almost 4,400 miles. The most notable addition that Murray made to the B&O system during his tenure was accomplished when a controlling interest in the Cincinnati, Hamilton & Dayton Railroad was purchased in 1909.

Like so many other lines that the B&O had picked up, the CH&D was something of a down-and-out operation. Chartered in 1846 as the Cincinnati & Hamilton Railroad, its name was soon changed to Cincinnati, Hamilton & Dayton to reflect goals beyond Hamilton. An extension to Dayton opened in 185, just as the Dayton & Michigan Railroad was laying track north of Dayton to Toledo. The D&M finished its line to Toledo in 1859, and the CH&D leased it in 1863. The Cincinnati–Toledo route formed the backbone of the CH&D as it took over several smaller lines, but the CH&D endured several years of financial distress before it was completely taken over by the B&O in 1917.

Oscar Murray resigned as B&O's president in 1910 to become chairman of the board. The name of his successor would soon become synonymous with that of the Baltimore & Ohio, and the company would take its place among America's legendary railroads.

DANIEL WILLARD'S B&O

Daniel Willard began life in 1861 as the son of a family of Vermont farmers. Although he was a hard-working youth, he was not inclined toward agriculture as an occupation. His interests gravitated toward railroading, and he entered the field as a track worker on the Vermont Central Railroad in 1879. Shortly, Willard was at work on locomotives as a fireman before being promoted to engineer. His career took him west where he rose through the management ranks to become a division superintendent on the Soo Line.

While on the Soo, Daniel Willard was a subordinate of general manager Frederick Underwood. When Underwood became B&O's general manager in 1899, he brought Willard along with him. Both Underwood and Willard would move to the Erie Railroad a couple of years later but during his brief tenure, Willard became familiar with many people on B&O's operating staff as well as with much of the road's infrastructure.

After working for the Erie, Willard went to the Chicago, Burlington & Quincy in 1904 as operating vice president. He held that position for six years until he was offered the presidency of the B&O in 1910. Having established his reputation as a proficient manager, Willard was probably one of the best choices the B&O

board could have made. Their judgement would be proven correct over the ensuing three decades.

During the first years of his administration, Willard did not add any new lines to the B&O, but instead concentrated on beefing up the existing system. As a man with plenty of hands-on operating experience, Willard saw many bottlenecks that impeded the flow of traffic over the railroad. Although several million dollars had been spent during the first decade of the twentieth century to rebuild the railroad's physical plant, there was still much to be done.

Among Willard's improvements were the addition of many miles of second main track between Philadelphia and Chicago. This included the construction of a new double-track bridge across the Susquehanna River at Perryville, Maryland, and the replacement of Sand Patch Tunnel in southwest Pennsylvania. But the most extensive undertaking of all was the elimination of the Doe Gully Tunnel west of Martinsburg, West Virginia.

In this area, the B&O main line ran along the south bank of the Potomac River from Cherry Run to Patterson Creek, West Virginia. The track followed the river as it made several tight bends over a short distance, and compounding this operating headache was the single-track Doe Gully Tunnel. Trains would be lined up at both ends of the tunnel waiting their turn to pass through. The solution to this obstruction was the Magnolia Cutoff.

Construction of the cutoff began in 1913 and involved two large bridges, four tunnels, and several long cuts and fills. Doe Gully Tunnel was "daylighted" (that is, the tunnel dynamited away), and four main tracks were laid through the resulting cut. West of the new cut, the new line followed a straighter and more level alignment, crossing the Potomac River twice. Traffic began moving over the cutoff in 1914, but the old main line remained in local service for nearly 50 more years.

Other Willard-inspired improvements included the purchase of new locomotives and rolling stock. Larger and more powerful locomotives were delivered while all-steel passenger and freight cars began to arrive.

As the B&O was busy putting its house in order, natural disaster struck a large area served by the railroad. During the last week of March 1913, three powerful air masses converged over the Ohio Valley bringing torrential rainfall to the region. The rain continued to fall

The Cleveland, Lorain & Wheeling stretched from Cleveland and Lorain to Wheeling, West Virginia, and came under B&O control in 1909. It provided B&O with a constant source of business, as the primary business was coal moving from West Virginia and southern Ohio to the docks at Lorain on Lake Erie. However, on this day in June 1957 at WC Tower, Warwick, Ohio, Class S-1a (2-10-2) No. 537 is heading a mixed bag of freight from Willard southward to Holloway, Ohio. The train is moving around the connection off the Chicago main. *Herbert H. Harwood Jr.*

Dayton, Ohio, was a major source of business on B&O's Cincinnati–Toledo main, as no less than six General Motors manufacturing plants resided in Dayton. These two southbound Electro-Motive F3As are crossing the Great Miami River on trackage of the Dayton Union Railway in November 1959. The tracks through downtown were jointly owned by the B&O, NYC, PRR, and Erie. Looming at lower right in the distance is the tower of Dayton Union Station at which stands the northbound *Cincinnatian*. Richard D. Acton Sr.

for five days. Much of the ground was still frozen, and the runoff caused streams and rivers to run over their banks flooding much of Indiana and Ohio. Hundreds of people lost their lives and tens of thousands lost their homes. Property damage was tallied in millions of dollars.

The railroads of the afflicted area were practically wiped out. The B&O sustained $3 million of damage to its property, with lost revenues totaling about half that amount. Over 170 miles of main line were destroyed while eleven major bridges were washed away and several more heavily damaged. Facilities at Wheeling, Marietta, Zanesville, Columbus, and Cincinnati were particularly hard hit by the floodwaters. The Parkersburg–Cincinnati main line was out of service for twelve days

and the St. Louis line west of Cincinnati was closed for a month. Throughout the crisis, Daniel Willard worked in the field, personally directing the recovery. The rebuilding of the railroad went on for many months with some repair work lasting into the following year.

Once the debacle of the 1913 flood had passed, the B&O resumed the expansion of its system. In 1916 the mileage of the national rail network would hit its high of 254,000 miles before beginning a long steady decline (with the exception of a slight increase in the late 1920s). In contrast, the B&O's mileage would continue to grow for another decade.

Among the most notable of Willard-era expansions was the formal takeover of the Cincinnati, Hamilton & Dayton. In 1909, B&O President Oscar Murray had arranged for the

when the B&O leased it in 1890. It ran south to Weston where the line split for Pickens and Richwood, mining towns at the ends of the branches. These branches and their connecting lines accounted for 60 percent of B&O's coal traffic.

After the B&O purchased the WV&P in 1912, it picked up another line in 1917—the Coal & Coke Railroad, a 200-mile line that ran from Elkins to Charleston, crossing both WV&P lines along the way. This network of lines in central West Virginia became the heart the railroad's coal business.

THE FIRST WORLD WAR

In the summer of 1914, war erupted across Europe, but most Americans did not want their country involved in what they perceived to be a foreign problem. The conflict quickly deteriorated into a stalemate, and the U.S. was slowly drawn into it as Britain and France came to depend on America for food, manufactured goods, and other supplies. To help American industry cope with the demands being placed upon it, President Woodrow Wilson created a committee of business leaders called the Council of National Defense. Daniel Willard accepted an invitation to join the committee in 1916, and in March 1917 he was elected chairman of the council.

As factory output of war materials grew, traffic levels on the nation's railroads rose rapidly. The shortage of workers became so acute that many retirees were called back to work. In this climate of full employment, the operating unions felt they were in a position to demand the standard ten-hour workday be reduced to eight hours and that they receive overtime pay for any work performed after eight hours. Railroad management refused their claims, and the issue came to a head. The four largest operating unions threatened to strike on Labor Day 1916.

President Wilson tried to mediate a settlement and asked Congress to draw up legislation that both unions and railroads would find acceptable. Congress responded by passing the Adamson Act granting labor their demand for an eight-hour workday but denying their claim for overtime pay. With the passage of the new law, the unions thought they had won. Union leaders cancelled their strike, but the railroads then claimed the Adamson Act was unconstitutional, and they took the new law to court to have it revoked. The unions called for another strike on March 17, 1917.

railroad to acquire the CH&D in seven years. Unfortunately, the CH&D was financially weak, and the red ink rose even after the floodwaters had receded. At its apex in 1915, the CH&D had been a 1,000-mile railroad, but by the time the B&O absorbed it in 1917, the CH&D had been trimmed to about 400 miles. Reorganized as the Toledo & Cincinnati Railroad, the most important lines were the main line between its namesake cities and a branch from Dayton that ran to Wellston in the coal-producing region of southern Ohio.

Also critical to B&O's expansion into coal fields during the Willard era were two branches that ran south from the Parkersburg main line, at Grafton and at Clarksburg, West Virginia. The branch from Clarksburg was known as the West Virginia & Pittsburgh

Under the administration of Daniel Willard, B&O made a number of major improvements to the flow of traffic over the railroad. One such improvement was the construction of the Magnolia Cutoff in 1913–14. The new line ran between Orleans Road and Okonoko (about two miles west of Paw Paw, West Virginia). In January 1984 a westbound empty coal train is exiting the Randolph Tunnel. Four tunnels and two large bridges were constructed for the cutoff. *Robert S. Kaplan*

At this point, Daniel Willard stepped in to arbitrate the dispute. With a reputation for being an efficient manager who had worked his way up through the ranks, Willard held the respect of both railroad management and the union membership. As the Supreme Court deliberated the legality of the Adamson Act, Willard was able to placate the union leadership long enough to avoid a nationwide rail strike, which could have been devastating to the war effort. The high court upheld the legality of the Adamson Act, and the confrontation was resolved for the time being. America's railroads continued moving people and freight as the nation teetered on the brink of war.

When Congress declared war on Germany

on April 6, 1917, the full weight of America was thrown into the war effort. Young men rushed to enlist in the armed forces, further aggravating the labor shortage confronting the country's industries. The Allied situation in Europe had become desperate, and war supplies were being forwarded to Eastern seaports at a frenzied pace. The railroads were not ready for the dramatic increase in traffic, and the national rail system was becoming paralyzed. As a railroad that served three of the most important ports on the East Coast (Baltimore, Philadelphia, and New York) the Baltimore & Ohio had its hands full with its share of the avalanche of people and goods.

The situation had become desperate by the spring of 1917 and as chairman of the Council of National Defense, Daniel Willard called a conference of the nation's railroad presidents in New York City. The purpose was to coordinate the efforts of the railroads in order to relieve the traffic jam. In spite of the railroads' efforts, things continued to get worse.

By the end of 1917, the federal government moved to take over operation of the railroads. President Wilson announced the implementation of the Federal Possession and Control Act on December 26, 1917, and appointed William G. McAdoo as director-general of the United States Railroad Administration. McAdoo was Secretary of the Treasury, and his railroad experience included the construction of the Hudson & Manhattan tunnels between New Jersey and New York City.

Daniel Willard remained the chairman of the Council of National Defense, but the body was nothing more than an advisory commission and had little influence as to how the USRA carried out its work. Although Willard was still the president of the B&O, he had no authority over the actual operation of the railroad; USRA called all the shots. The wages of the nation's railroad employees were raised by the USRA. Freight and passenger rates were also increased, though not enough to keep pace with the rising costs of coal and other supplies. Operating ratios (the percentage of revenues consumed by operating expenses) climbed dramatically.

When private control was returned on March 1, 1920, the country's railroads were in poor shape. Payments by the USRA fell short of operating expenses. Rolling stock was worn out, and maintenance of track and structures had been neglected. For much of the industry, the takeover ended up an economic disaster.

THE BIG BIRTHDAY PARTY

During the years leading up to the war, the B&O had made many improvements to its own infrastructure, so it tended to fare better than many other lines did under government control. As the 1920s began, the B&O found itself in the best position to compete with the three other Northeastern trunk lines (namely PRR, NYC, and Erie) that it had ever enjoyed.

The B&O marked its centennial in 1927 and celebrated the occasion by orchestrating a big outdoor exposition. The Fair of the Iron Horse was held at a specially built site at Halethorpe, Maryland, near Baltimore. In addition to commemorating B&O's birthday, Daniel Willard wanted to showcase the achievements of the entire railroad industry to the public.

Several other railroads participated in the event including long-time B&O rivals PRR and NYC. The latest locomotives and rolling stock were displayed alongside many pieces of early railroad equipment while many other displays showed the advances that had been made in the realm of safety and traffic capacity. A pageant depicting two centuries of transportation history was choreographed and played for the duration of the fair.

The exhibition was open for 23 days during September and October. Admission was free and total attendance topped 1.25 million visitors. Although the exhibition cost more than $1 million to sponsor, the value of the positive public relations that the industry reaped was immeasurable.

THE FINAL ADDITIONS

The last major additions to B&O's system map were made during the late 1920s and early 1930s. The Transportation Act of 1920 had put control of the railroads back into the private sector but also gave the ICC more regulatory muscle. The act also called for the consolidation of the nation's railroads into a smaller group of larger systems—the rationale being to merge weaker roads with more stable lines while still preserving competition. B&O made it to the short list of major systems that would survive.

The ICC planning process turned out to be controversial and confused and was never

As part of its centennial celebration, B&O introduced its now-famous blue Centennial china—later referred to as its "Centenary" pattern—which depicted various aspects of B&O evolution. Centenary china would be found on B&O passenger trains right up to Amtrak's 1971 assumption of most of the nation's intercity passenger trains. This pattern became a much sought-after collectible. *Collection of Mike McBride*

implemented, but B&O would pick up some of the lines that the plan had allocated to the railroad. B&O's share of the Reading Company (which in turn controlled the Jersey Central) was increased, thus tightening B&O's grip on the route to New York City. Also, the B&O entered new territory in western New York State during 1929 when it bought a controlling interest in the Buffalo, Rochester & Pittsburgh. Connecting with B&O's Pittsburgh & Western at Butler, Pennsylvania, the BR&P ran north to Rochester, on Lake Ontario, and Buffalo, at the eastern tip of Lake Erie.

B&O also bought the Buffalo & Susquehanna, a rural line that extended across the north central portion of the Keystone State from the BR&P at Du Bois, Pennsylvania. Willard was attempting to assemble a northern route across Pennsylvania to reach New York, New Jersey, and New England markets. A new line was to be built to join the BR&P/B&S with the northwest end of Reading at Williamsport. The BR&P and B&S both became part of the B&O in 1932, but the business environment of the 1930s prevented completion of the project.

Back in Maryland, B&O was buying up shares of another hometown railroad, the Western Maryland Railway. WM roughly paralleled the B&O from Baltimore to Cumberland and Connellsville, Pennsylvania, but took a more northerly route through Hagerstown, Maryland. Beyond Cumberland the WM divided into two lines: one to Connellsville where it connected to the Pittsburgh & Lake Erie and the other into the West Virginia coal fields.

Chartered in Baltimore in 1863, the Western Maryland Rail Road first built northwest from the city to Westminster and Union Bridge, Maryland. The City of Baltimore controlled the WM until it sold its holdings to George Gould in 1902. Heading west from Hagerstown, the WM in 1906 completed a line to Cumberland where it connected with a coal road, the West Virginia Central & Pittsburgh Railway. The WVC&P became part of the WM in 1910, and the new Connellsville Extension was opened in 1912.

Gould's empire fell on hard times, and in 1908 the WM entered receivership. It was reorganized as the Western Maryland Rail*way* in 1910 when John D. Rockefeller took control of the line. B&O bought Rockefeller's share of the WM in 1927, giving it 43 percent of the road. The ICC stepped in and charged B&O with violating anti-trust laws. B&O was ordered to sell its WM holdings, but the financial turmoil of the 1930s made such a sale difficult. B&O finally placed its WM stock in a non-voting trust where it would remain for several years.

At the western end of the B&O, the ICC allowed the purchase the Cincinnati, Indianapolis & Western Railroad in 1926. The 320-mile CI&W had been part of the Cincinnati, Hamilton & Dayton empire before its dismemberment. The railroad joined B&O's Cincinnati–Toledo main line at Hamilton, Ohio, near Cincinnati and ran westward through Indianapolis and to Springfield, Illinois, where it met the former Ohio & Mississippi line between Beardstown and Shawneetown.

B&O's ties with the Reading Railroad dated from the turn of the century when rival Pennsylvania Railroad acquired control of the B&O. The Reading (and Reading-controlled Jersey Central) affiliation was strengthened by the Transportation Act of 1920 which foresaw the need for railroad consolidation on a national level. The B&O/RDG/CNJ triumvirate lasted nearly to the end of the Reading and Jersey Central, both of which were swept into the 1976 formation of Conrail. In this scene at Hammond, Indiana, in July 1964, B&O and Reading locomotives lead an eastbound freight through State Line interlocking. Pooled Reading power was common on East Coast–Chicago freights. *Jim Boyd*

On a spring day in 1962, Electro-Motive GP9s lead the daily Springfield–Decatur, Illinois, freight past the Chicago & Illinois Midland yard in Springfield as one of C&IM's switchers pauses during its yard duties. The B&O train is en route from the former-Alton Railroad's (Gulf, Mobile & Ohio after 1947) Ridgely Yard on the north side of town to Avenue Tower on the city's southeast side where the train will enter home rails. B&O and GM&O shared the facility, which also hosted B&O power assigned to the Beardstown, Illinois, branch. *Dave Ingles*

In 1929 the Chicago & Alton Railroad was sold to B&O interests at a foreclosure sale and was reorganized as the Alton Railroad in 1931. The Alton ran between Chicago and St. Louis and Kansas City and connected with the B&O at Chicago, St. Louis, and Springfield, putting it in the unique position of being the only East Coast-based railroad to operate beyond usual east-west gateways of Chicago and St. Louis to Kansas City, which rankled some Western rail-roads. The B&O kept the Alton until 1942, but operated it as a separate company although with some B&O locomotives and rolling stock. A Baltimore–Kansas City through route (via Springfield) never materialized.

As Willard was making these final acquisi-tions, the nation's economy was collapsing in the wake of the stockmarket crash of October 1929. The 1920s had been prosperous, but the 1930s would bring years of hardship.

B&O ownership of the Alton Railroad between 1929 and 1942 presented the B&O an opportunity to form a main through route between the East Coast and Kansas City via the Springfield, Illinois, gateway. However, this scenario never realized its full potential, probably in part because of the Great Depression. Regardless, B&O's presence on the Alton Route was unmistakable, as illustrated in this 1939 scene at Springfield of the Chicago–St. Louis *Alton Limited* striding into the depot behind EA/EB diesel set No. 51. Even as late as 1999, B&O-style color-light signals could still be seen along the old Alton Route Chicago–St. Louis main line. *Collection of Louis A. Marre*

In an effort to bypass the steep grades on the B&O's Pittsburgh & Western main west of Pittsburgh, the B&O sought trackage rights on the Pittsburgh & Lake Erie Railroad. In 1934, 58 miles of trackage rights were secured from McKeesport to New Castle, Pennsylvania. On June 26, 1983, an eastbound empty train passes P&LE's primary yard at McKees Rocks. *Steve Salamon*

THE GREAT DEPRESSION

As the Great Depression swept in, business across America slowed as company after company declared bankruptcy. Factories closed as orders for their products dwindled. The raw materials to make the products were no longer needed, and rail traffic dropped quickly while revenues shrank. During the 1920s, many railroads, including B&O, had purchased other lines and made expensive improvements to existing lines. When the Depression struck, falling income could not cover this debt and rising operating costs. Railroads had also lost a substantial portion of passenger and freight traffic during the 1920s as public roads improved. The public was traveling more by automobile and bus while industry was shipping more by truck.

By late 1932, a financial crisis was developing as the B&O posted a $6 million deficit, meanwhile facing over $63 million of 20-year bonds that would mature on March 1,1933. Willard was able to avert default by negotiating a loan from the Reconstruction Finance Corporation, a federal agency created to assist failing businesses. The railroad was able make ends meet for five more years before it had to get another loan from the RFC in 1938. The B&O managed to stay out of receivership until business improved at the end of the decade.

Despite the Depression, the B&O did make some improvements. In 1934, it secured 58 miles of trackage rights over the Pittsburgh

& Lake Erie between McKeesport and New Castle, Pennsylvania to bypass the steepest grades and twisting route of its own Pittsburgh & Western line between those points. The agreement was laced with a bit of irony, because the B&O had passed up an opportunity to buy into the P&LE back in the 1870s.

Despite B&O's precarious financial status during the Depression years, some new equipment was purchased. Under the direction of Colonel George H. Emerson, General Superintendent of Motive Power, 46 new locomotives were acquired between 1930 and 1940—nine steam engines and 37 diesels. Seven of the steam locomotives were equipped with experimental water-tube boilers to enhance performance, but the ratio of new steam to new diesel was a testimony to the B&O's faith in the newfangled diesel power. Thirteen of the new diesels were passenger units and were the first self-contained streamlined diesel passenger locomotives on America's railroads.

Air-conditioned passenger equipment was introduced in 1930, and B&O's first air-conditioned train entered service in 1931. Two experimental lightweight passenger trains debuted in 1935, one between Washington and Jersey City (the *Royal Blue*) and the other on B&O's Alton Railroad between Chicago and St. Louis (the *Abraham Lincoln*).

DANIEL WILLARD STEPS DOWN

As America struggled through the Depression, other parts of the world were in upheaval. Germany was rearming and flexing its muscle. In the final years of the 1930s, war was about to engulf Europe again. America was focused on events in Europe, but Japan had also been waging a military campaign in China since 1931. When the European war began in 1939, American industry still wasn't up to full capacity, but B&O revenues began to rebound. The fall of France and the Battle of Britain in 1940 accelerated industrial output as the U.S. came to the aid of the British.

As the B&O became busy again moving coal and iron ore to the steel mills of the Ohio

Valley and the south shore of Lake Erie, Daniel Willard celebrated his 80th birthday in January 1941. Willard had served the B&O for 31 years and decided the time had come to let someone else run the railroad to which he had dedicated much of his life. Upon his resignation from the presidency, Willard was elected chairman of the board, a position he would hold until his death in July 1942. During his presidential term, Willard had expanded the B&O from 4,400 miles in 1910 to its zenith of 6,371 miles in 1937. As America edged towards involvement in the war, Roy B. White took the president's chair in June 1941.

WORLD WAR II

Many Americans had come to realize that their country would soon be involved in the European war, but the Japanese attack on Pearl Harbor meant the U.S. would fight a war on two fronts. By early 1942, industry was working toward full capacity, and traffic levels on the railroads were the highest they had been since 1930. Railroads shifted from years of slow traffic or no traffic to more business than they could handle.

The rail industry of 1942 had evolved considerably since World War I, and this time it was able to rise to the demands of war. Locomotives could pull more and rolling stock could carry more. Track and signals could accommodate longer and heavier trains. Although under tighter wartime regulation, the railroads would remain under private management during the World War II.

Over 17,000 B&O employees joined the armed services during the war, and 201 died in service to their country. To fill vacated positions, B&O hired thousands of new employees, many of them women, while many retirees also returned to work.

In early 1942, German submarines disrupted shipping along the Atlantic coast and in the Gulf of Mexico, forcing vital oil traffic to be moved by rail. B&O moved its share of oil trains, handling about 850 tank cars over its system on an average day in 1943.

New equipment was hard to come by, but the War Production Board did allow the B&O to buy 30 new steam locomotives in 1944–45. These would be B&O's biggest—and last—steam locomotives. But, new diesel road freight locomotives being delivered at the same time spoke of a new era for railroading.

The high levels of traffic and revenues during the early 1940s helped the B&O balance sheet. The corporate structure of the railroad was simplified as many subsidiary companies were consolidated into the B&O. The number of subsidiaries dropped from 107 to 70.

The tide of the war turned in favor of the Allies in 1944. Victory in Europe was achieved in May 1945, and Japan surrendered in September. Peacetime would return to America, but with it came new challenges for the B&O and U.S. railroads as a whole.

B&O acquired its famed EM-1-class 2-8-8-4 steam locomotives from Baldwin just as World War II was winding down. Alas, the future of steam on the B&O—and on railroads nationwide—had become finite by the close of the war as diesels took on new importance. On the Lake Branch circa 1950, a southbound EM-1 on a coal drag meets its fate in the form of an Alco switcher at Chardou, Ohio. *Herbert H. Harwood Jr.*

INSET: Artwork from the post-World War II era depicted a dynamic Baltimore & Ohio where giant steam was still king of freight transport while modern diesels sped passengers throughout the system. *Collection of Herbert H. Harwood Jr.*

ABOVE: Amalgamation and merger were keywords in the twilight years of B&O, and this scene at Thomas Viaduct illustrates those very aspects of the Baltimore & Ohio as three Electro-Motive diesels—B&O GP30 No. 6917, GP7 No. 5629 in Chessie System colors, and Western Maryland SD35 No. 7434—lead a westbound freight over the historic span near Elkridge, Maryland, in April, 1977. The largest bridge in the U.S. at the time of its construction in 1835, Thomas Viaduct was also the first curved masonry bridge. *Steve Salamon*

CHAPTER 4

The Modern B&O

1945-1987: THE FINAL DECADES

The end of World War II also marked the end of a few prosperous years for the B&O. Troop trains brought the veterans home, but when they got off the train there was a car waiting for them at the station. B&O still moved a lot of coal and steel, but the end of hostilities meant it would be moving less.

Once again B&O was facing many of the same challenges it had before the war. But armed with the postwar optimism shared by many railroads, B&O bought new passenger and freight equipment during the postwar years even as revenues fell. B&O was still one of the primary coal-hauling railroads of the East, but continued with the conversion of its locomotive fleet to diesel power to take advantage of the enormous savings made possible by dieselization. In spite of the many improvements that it made to its physical plant after the war, the B&O could do little to stop the exodus of its traffic base.

During the 1930s and 1940s, the Army Corps of Engineers built several dams, locks, and flood-control projects along the Ohio River and many of its tributaries. As a benefit of these improvements, the transport of bulk commodities such as coal, stone, and chemicals by river became more reliable and economical. Although barges move at a much slower speed than a freight car, the cost of shipping by river is much less than rail.

Federal and state highway construction programs pushed new roads across the country. The public took to the roads in their own cars, and the trucking industry went looking for new business. Few people who had heard of the Wright Brothers and their "flying machine" in 1903 were aware of how far the basic principles of their work would be taken over the next half-century. By the 1920s, public air travel had become a fact, although it was for the limited few who were endowed with the means to buy a plane ticket and the nerve (or ignorance) to board the plane.

Things changed with the end of the war. Air travel became more commonplace as pilots, mechanics, and cargo planes were released from the armed forces. New airliners with more seats were being built, and ticket prices became more attractive.

In the face of this new level and variety of competition, B&O President Roy White did his best to reverse—or at least reduce—the slide in passenger and freight revenues. New technologies were applied to reduce operating expenses. Centralized traffic control (CTC), which allowed a single dispatcher to do the work of several tower and station operators, was installed on segments of B&O's busiest main lines. The installation of continuous welded rail reduced track maintenance costs.

As trucks ate away at B&O's freight traffic, new marketing services were inaugurated to retain business. "Sentinel" freight service was introduced in 1947 to guarantee delivery dates for carload freight shipments by employing a new teletype system to track car movements. Less-than-carload (LCL) lading received similar treatment when "Timesaver" service was introduced in 1950.

B&O's mileage was also trimmed during the late 1940s after the ICC consolidation plan of the 1920s had been made irrelevant by the Depression. The Alton Railroad was allowed to fall into receivership, and the Gulf, Mobile & Ohio acquired it in 1947.

The Korean War broke out in June 1950 and both freight and passenger traffic began to increase as the U.S. mobilized its armed forces. That same year there would be a change in B&O's boardroom.

Capitol Limited Columbian Shenandoah*

For information and reservations, call
L. L. CHAMBERLAIN
Passenger Representative
STerling 8100

53,000 employees. By 1960 the railroad would be only a bit smaller at 5,900 miles, but would be operated by 33,000 workers. Simpson's term brought many improvements to the B&O, but annual revenues hit their peak year in 1956 and fell for the next six years.

B&O still made a vigorous effort to change with the times. It initiated trailer-on-flatcar "piggyback" service in 1954, years before it was widely called "intermodal." The conversion to diesel power was completed in 1958, and track maintenance was mechanized with machines that could perform the work of dozens of manual laborers.

More excess trackage was cast aside in late 1955 as much of the Buffalo & Susquehanna was sold to a shortline operator. A good portion

THE NOT-SO-NIFTY FIFTIES

Like many other U.S. railroads, B&O entered the post-World War II era with much hope for passenger service. Reflecting this optimism, B&O took delivery of new streamlined rolling stock in the late 1940s and early 1950s, including new "Strata-Dome" cars. This ink blotter (an unheard-of desk accessory today, but common in the era of fountain pens) touted the new glass-topped cars, which entered service on the *Capitol Limited*, *Columbian*, and—on certain days only—the *Shenandoah*. All were Chicago–Jersey City trains. *Collection of William F. Howes Jr.*

Twelve years after he replaced Daniel Willard as B&O's president, Roy White announced his retirement in September 1953. Succeeding White was Executive Vice President Howard E. Simpson, who became B&O's sixteenth president. Simpson inherited a 6,200-mile railroad that was run by about

B&O was not immune to the recession of the late 1950s and the general downturn in freight and passenger business after World War II owing to increased competition from automobiles and the trucking industry. In 1958, B&O finally conceded the Washington–New York passenger market to rival Pennsylvania Railroad, discontinuing all passenger service east of Baltimore. On April 22, 1958, the westbound *Royal Blue* makes one of its final crossings of the Susquehanna River on the Royal Blue Line. *Collection of William F. Howes Jr.*

of B&S track was washed away in 1942, isolating the northern portion of the line. The island railroad became the Wellsville, Addison & Galeton Railroad.

But the onslaught of competition continued unabated through the 1950s. By mid-decade, many railroads were in trouble, particularly in the Northeast where numerous lines overlapped and duplicated service. Hoping to hang on to the traffic they had picked up during the war, many railroads invested heavily in new passenger equipment. In the long run, their efforts proved to be futile, as most travelers in the postwar years would come to prefer the convenience of the auto or the speed of the airplane. The Pennsylvania and New York Central railroads were hit particularly hard as their vast passenger operations incurred ever-growing deficits.

B&O didn't have any better luck than its neighbors when it came to passenger trains, but it was fortunate in that it had far fewer of them, nor did it run a big fleet of commuter trains. Nonetheless, B&O's passenger deficits continued to grow. Schedules were trimmed greatly during the late 1950s, and all passenger service east of Baltimore ceased in April 1958.

THE BATTLE FOR B&O

Convinced that they couldn't regain traffic lost to other modes of transportation, railroad executives looked for ways to further reduce expenses. Most agreed that merging to create bigger systems (which, in theory, would be more efficient) was essential to the survival of the railroad industry. The Depression and the World War II had put the consolidation of the nation's railroads on hold, but the industry began to coalesce in the mid-1950s.

In 1957 the Nashville, Chattanooga & St. Louis merged with the Louisville & Nashville Railroad in the first of a long series of rail mergers. By the end of the century the number of Class One railroads would be reduced from over one hundred to less than a dozen.

As the merger movement gained momentum, the Pennsylvania Railroad shocked the industry in 1957 by proposing merger talks with its principal foe, the New York Central. NYC resisted initially, then proposed a three-way union with the Chesapeake & Ohio Railroad and the B&O. However, C&O's board of directors had their own agenda for the B&O and in June 1960 went to the Interstate Commerce Commission seeking approval to buy

In a scene typical of B&O freight operations in the diesel era, an Electro-Motive F3 and F7 still clad in the classic blue/gray/black livery highball west on the Pittsburgh–Chicago main line at Fostoria, Ohio, during the summer of 1961. In 1999, this depot would still be serving passenger trains, albeit Amtrak, not B&O. *Dave Ingles*

The B&O/C&O affiliation was plainly evident throughout the 1960s. At Seymour, Indiana, on the Cincinnati–St. Louis main line in March 1964, C&O influence is apparent in some of the F-units powering the two trains meeting. B&O F7 4464 leads a C&O F7B and a B&O F7B on eastbound train 94 while a C&O F7A—wearing a thankfully brief-lived experimental black and white scheme—is partially visible on the opposing train at far right. *Dave Ingles*

controlling interest in the B&O.

By the end of the 1950s, B&O's financial troubles were deepening. The railroad reported large deficits for 1960 and 1961. Howard Simpson was elected chairman of the board and chief executive officer in May 1961, and in June of that year, Jervis Langdon Jr. became the last president of an independent Baltimore & Ohio Railroad.

The C&O was a tidewater coal road that ran westward across Virginia from Newport News. It covered much of the southern half of West Virginia with branches tapping into the mines. At Ashland, Kentucky, C&O's main route split in three directions, with one line headed to the coal docks at Toledo, another to Chicago via Cincinnati, and a third to Lexington, Kentucky, to connect with the Louisville & Nashville.

Unlike B&O and NYC, the C&O was making a respectable living hauling coal for export and domestic use. C&O stockholders knew that the NYC would benefit more from a union with C&O than would the C&O, so they rejected the

proposal. Rather, C&O saw the B&O alone as a better merger partner. Between them, the two roads carried the majority of West Virginia's coal production, with B&O covering the northern half of the state while the C&O served much of the rest. The C&O also saw the B&O as a better connection in the industrial Midwest because it didn't field as many costly branchlines as did the Central.

By the end of 1960, C&O announced it held 30 percent of B&O stock, and its stake in the B&O (and therefore Western Maryland, Reading, and Jersey Central as well) rose to 70 percent in the early months of 1961 as both roads awaited a decision from the ICC. Approval of the merger came on the last day of 1962. The order took effect on February 4, 1963, and the C&O took control of the B&O on that same day although they did not formally merge.

Realizing its bid to merge with the C&O had failed, NYC turned back to the Pennsy. They would eventually combine in 1968 to become the ill-fated Penn Central Corporation.

C&O TAKES THE THROTTLE

For the first years following C&O takeover, one could hardly tell the B&O belonged to another railroad. Each company conducted its business under its own name and retained its own logo, but they shared a combined annual report beginning in 1964. A family resemblance emerged in terms of livery worn by rolling stock and locomotives of the two railroads, although reporting marks indicated that everything still belonged to different lines.

Jervis Langdon resigned as B&O's president in 1964 and went to work for the Rock Island (like Leonor Loree 60 years earlier in 1904). He was succeeded on the B&O by a number of C&O men, the first being Walter Touhy.

As president of the C&O since 1948, Touhy played a key role in the 1963 buyout of the B&O. He held the presidency for only a year (1964–65) before relinquishing the post to Gregory S. DeVine. During DeVine's term, the gradual integration of B&O into the C&O continued. C&O held merger talks with another coal road, the Norfolk & Western, in the late 1960s. Agreement was reached and submitted to the ICC in 1966, but the collapse of Penn Central prompted C&O and N&W to drop the plan in 1971.

The ICC gave its approval in 1967 to complete the C&O/B&O takeover of the Western Maryland. As the "Wild Mary" was assimilated into C&O/B&O, a new corporate structure was created in 1972. The C&O, B&O, and WM began operating under a new unified identity, Chessie System, Inc., a holding company which controlled the three railroads. "Chessie System" was also adopted as the marketing name for the railroads, although each railroad still maintained its own corporate identity.

UNDER THE SIGN OF THE CAT

The Chessie name and logo traced its origins back to a C&O advertising campaign that began in 1933. C&O had chosen the work of artist Guido Gruenewald to publicize its air-conditioned sleeping cars. His etching portrayed a sleeping kitten named Chessie, after the railroad. The campaign proved popular with the public, and the sleeping kitten became the trademark of C&O passenger service well into the 1960s. The new Chessie System logo was stylized through a clever placement of the kitten's silhouette inside the letter C. Locomotives and rolling stock carried the Chessie logo as well as the reporting marks for the B&O, C&O, or WM.

An example of coordinated advertising by C&O and B&O following their post-1950s amalgamation. B&O had been a pioneer in "piggyback" intermodal service, inaugurating trailer-on-flatcar (TOFC or "TOFCEE," as it was marketed by B&O) in 1954. This comprehensive booklet illustrated how piggyback service worked and also provided schedules for B&O's *Trailer Jet* network. *Collection of Dave Ori*

THE CHESAPEAKE AND OHIO / BALTIMORE AND OHIO RAILROADS

PIGGYBACK

BALTIMORE AND OHIO RAILROAD

TRAILER SERVICE
COORDINATED RAIL-TRUCK ROUTES COAST-TO-COAST

A Modern, Flexible Transportation Service That Saves You Time and Money

Under the familiar countenance of the Washington Monument, Western Maryland SD40 7546 crosses the Potomac River in Washington, D.C. on January 23, 1977, at the head of a B&O freight out of Potomac Yard. *Steve Salamon*

In 1977 B&O celebrated its 150th anniversary. Although Chessie System didn't throw a big party like the one of 1927, it did host a series of excursion trains pulled by a steam locomotive that ran between various cities around the system.

The National Rail Passenger Corporation, better known as Amtrak, had been formed by Congress to take over most of the nation's remaining intercity rail passenger service on May 1, 1971, and B&O/C&O joined Amtrak. By that time the only B&O intercity passenger trains were running between Washington and Chicago and St. Louis and between Toledo and Cincinnati. None of these B&O routes were included in the initial Amtrak route structure on May 1, however a few months after the carrier's start-up, a new Amtrak train, the *Potomac Special*, began operating between Washington and Parkersburg, West Virginia. In 1976 the schedule was extended to Cincinnati for a few years—reviving the B&O name *Shenandoah*—until the train was cancelled in

1981 and ending all passenger operations on B&O's St. Louis route. At the same time Amtrak discontinued the Washington–Cincinnati run, it revived the *Capitol Limited* between Washington and Chicago. The new run followed the original B&O *Capitol Limited* route only between Washington and Pittsburgh, west of which it was combined with Amtrak's New York–Chicago *Broadway Limited* operating via the former PRR main line.

Even as the government relieved most of the railroads of their money-losing passenger trains, the rail industry was greatly concerned with the collapse of the Northeastern railroad network. Penn Central declared bankruptcy in 1970, and eventually six other lines followed suit, including Reading and Jersey Central. Chessie System management subsequently gave up on the New York market and sold off B&O's Reading stock in the early 1970s.

Intervention by the federal government came when Consolidated Rail Corporation (Conrail) was formed to assume the operations

continued on page 66

The new Chessie System colors and markings debuted in 1972 at Electro-Motive's 50th anniversary celebration at its LaGrange plant in west suburban Chicago. Considered one of the best of contemporary railroad liveries, the new image—partly prompted by safety considerations—was inspired by C&O's ever-popular Chessie the Cat marketing of yore. Three units wear the colors on a freight at Piqua, Ohio, in January 1985.
Kirk Reynolds

The face of the B&O in its final years of truly separate identity shows in this view of a freight at Second Street Junction in Dayton, Ohio, in October 1974. *David P. Oroszi*

The Baltimore & Ohio Chicago Terminal
B&O's Freight and Passenger Operations in Chicagoland

A B&OCT switcher leads a transfer through the complex interlocking plant at State Line Tower, Hammond, Indiana, during the summer of 1965. B&OCT's freight main line passed through State Line—intersection with the Erie Lackawanna, Norfolk & Western, Chesapeake & Ohio of Indiana, and Indiana Harbor Belt—between Hammond, Indiana, and Calumet Park, Illinois. *Dave Ingles*

The Baltimore & Ohio Chicago Terminal Railroad was a company separate from B&O proper, with all stock held by B&O. B&OCT's primary role was to collect and distribute freight in the Chicago area—freight traveling to or from B&O's main line into Chicago or between connecting carriers. In addition, B&OCT provided a path into downtown Chicago for B&O, Pere Marquette, Soo Line, and Chicago Great Western passenger trains.

B&OCT's earliest roots date from the 1867 formation of the La Salle & Chicago Railroad. That road's franchise was acquired by another company, Chicago & Great Western, which by 1885 had built a line extending east from Forest Park into downtown Chicago to serve as a terminal line for the Wisconsin Central and the Minnesota & North Western railroads (predecessors to Soo Line and CGW, respectively). Meanwhile, the Northern Pacific, controlled by financier Henry Villard, obtained lease control of the WC to provide an entry to Chicago. A new subsidiary, Chicago & Northern Pacific, acquired the C&GW in 1890.

Finding C&GW's passenger depot at Polk Street inadequate, Villard bought a coal yard at Wells and Harrison streets in 1889 on which he built the ornate Grand Central Station, opened on December 10, 1890. Designed by Solon Spencer Beman, the architect responsible for George Pullman's company town on Chicago's South Side, Grand Central—topped by an imposing clock tower with an 11,000-pound bell tolling the hours—exuded the style of a Norman castle. WC passenger trains first used the depot—which was why it was sometimes known as Wisconsin Central Station—and B&O passenger trains began using Grand Central in 1891, 17 years after the B&O arrived in Chicago. The Chicago extension had reached the Illinois Central at Brookdale, in South Chicago, in 1874 and from then to 1901, B&O trains used IC tracks between Brookdale and downtown Chicago where, over the years, B&O operated out of various lakefront depots. Looking for a larger terminal, B&O shifted its passenger trains to Grand Central in 1891 using rights over Rock Island and the Pennsylvania

Railroad between South Chicago and Western Avenue to reach the C&NP. In 1892, Chicago Great Western passenger trains began serving the depot, and in 1903 Pere Marquette became a tenant. While La Salle Street Station was under construction between 1900 and 1903, New York Central and Rock Island passenger trains also used Grand Central. In 1900 B&O leased, and eventually purchased, the stately depot and became the primary user.

During the same era, freight operations in the growing city had become severely congested, prompting B&O to negotiate an agreement with the Chicago & Calumet Terminal Railroad, one of several fledgling belt lines formed to expedite traffic through the area. Also backed by Villard interests, the C&CT had built a line from the B&O main line at Whiting, Indiana, to the Santa Fe at McCook, Illinois. C&CT intended to continue northward, but in 1896 it joined forces with the Chicago, Hammond & Western, predecessor of today's Indiana Harbor Belt, which planned a similar route. C&CT granted rights to the CH&W between Blue Island and McCook, and CH&W built a line, for joint use,

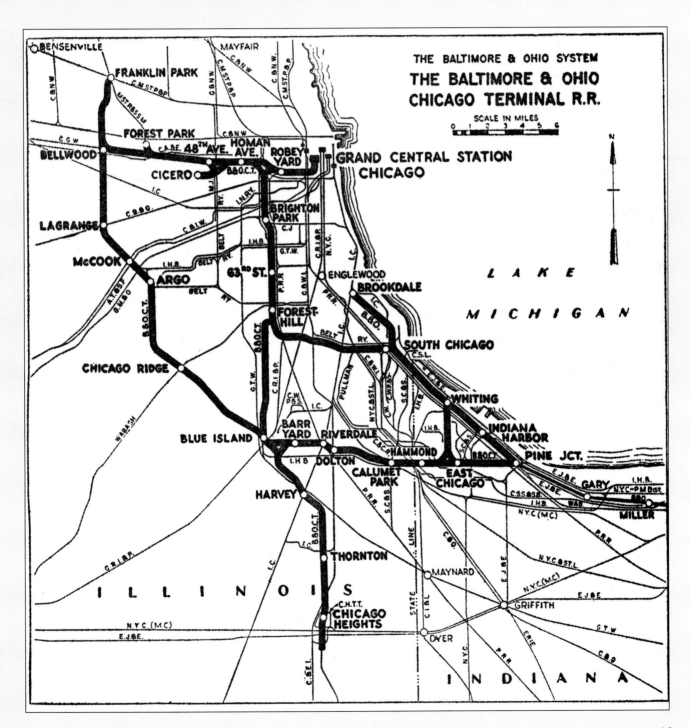

B&O and C&O passenger trains made a convoluted trip in and out of Chicago along a B&O/B&OCT routing that included some stretches of trackage rights. On a fall day in 1969, the eastbound *Gateway* is shown swinging off the B&OCT and onto Rock Island's Suburban Branch at Beverly Junction on Chicago's South Side. *Dave Ingles*

from McCook north to a connection with the Chicago, Milwaukee & St. Paul at Franklin Park. Thus was born an arrangement that endured into the 1980s, with B&OCT and IHB sharing the busy Blue Island–Franklin Park multiple-track main line.

Meanwhile, the C&NP was also expanding. In 1890, Villard interests helped build a line from the C&NP into Cicero. Next, C&NP obtained the Chicago Central Railway, which had built a line from downtown Chicago to Blue Island, connecting there with the C&CT. In the Panic of 1893, Villard was forced to surrender control of WC and C&NP. The latter was reorganized as the Chicago Terminal Transfer Railroad in 1897, and in 1898 it acquired control of C&CT and completed a line from Blue Island to Chicago

Heights. The CTTR was in receivership in 1910 when B&O purchased its stock and reorganized it as the B&OCT.

B&O saw advantages in owning its own terminal railroad in the Chicago area. B&OCT tracks formed an arc around the southern and western sides of the city and thus provided B&O with direct connections to almost every Class I and switching carrier in the Chicago area. B&OCT became one of three major Chicago switching lines (the others were IHB and Belt Railway of Chicago).

At its peak in the 1920s, B&OCT operated 78 route-miles and 365 track-miles, plus 42 miles of trackage rights. It interchanged with 34 railroads at 54 points, calling 90 or more crews to handle up to 3,500 cars a day. Roughly half of those cars were handled for B&O. The balance was traffic handled in intermediate switch runs between other carriers, or traffic moving between B&OCT-served sidings and connections other than B&O.

B&OCT's main line into downtown Chicago was 34 miles long, from NE Tower at Pine Junction to Grand Central Station. The portion between Pine Junction and Blue Island was used by most B&O through freights, which worked at Barr Yard. Beyond Blue Island, the main line turned due north to Western Avenue, then curved east past Robey Yard to Grand Central. From the wye at Western Avenue Junction, the Altenheim Branch (former C&GW) went west seven miles to Forest Park, connecting there with Soo Line and Chicago Great Western.

The joint B&OCT-IHB line between Blue Island and Franklin Park was known as the McCook Branch and was a very busy railroad—though mostly with IHB trains. B&OCT crews switched sidings between Blue Island and Argo and operated transfers to Chicago & North Western's Proviso Yard. The Chicago Heights Branch served many industries around Harvey and Thornton.

B&O passenger trains used the original B&O Chicago extension between Pine Junction and South Chicago, along Lake Michigan. West of South Chicago, trains used trackage rights over Rock Island's South Chicago Branch for 6.3 miles to Beverly Junction, then two miles of B&O-owned track to reach the B&OCT main at Forest Hill. C&O's ex-Pere Marquette passenger trains also used this routing, but entered B&O rails at Hick interlocking just west of Pine Junction. B&OCT crews switched freight customers along the passenger route, and through freights with no work at Barr Yard occasionally ran this way.

Inbound passenger trains usually backed into Grand Central from the wye at Western Avenue Junction, 3.7 miles from the depot. B&O trains shared Grand Central's eight stub tracks with passenger trains of Soo Line, Chicago Great Western, and C&O (ex-Pere Marquette routes only). CGW went freight-only in 1956 and Soo moved its last trains to Illinois Central's Central Station in 1963. By the late 1960s, only the *Capitol Limited,* the Washington–Chicago *Diplomat* (westbound only), the Chicago–Pittsburgh *Gateway* (eastbound only), and one pair of C&O trains remained. On November 8, 1969, these trains departed and arrived Grand Central for the last time, moving to North Western Station the next day. To reach that depot, B&O/C&O trains followed their traditional route into Chicago as far as Western Avenue Junction, from which they entered a C&NW branch that lead to North Western's main line a short distance to the north. These trains disappeared entirely with the coming of Amtrak in 1971, the same year that Grand Central Station was demolished.

Barr was the largest B&OCT freight yard. After a three-year expansion project completed in 1948, Barr consisted of eastbound and westbound receiving yards holding 345 and 500 cars respectively, and east- and westbound classification yards with respective capacities of 1,144 and 1,209 cars. Also at Barr were a turntable and engine facilities, repair tracks, and a stockcar servicing yard. Barr Yard performed a dual role as the main yard for B&O road-haul freight traffic in and out of Chicago as well as the classification point for traffic handled by BO&CT.

The next busiest B&OCT yard was at Robey Street, just east of Western Avenue Junction. This yard was used to service industrial spurs and numerous freight stations and team tracks on the west side of downtown Chicago. Into the 1970s, most eastbound B&O road trains were dispatched from Robey Yard, filling out at Forest Hill or Barr Yard. A 33-stall enginehouse served B&OCT switchers and B&O freight and passenger locomotives. B&O passenger equipment was serviced at nearby Lincoln Avenue coach yards.

B&OCT had eight other yards that served industrial and commercial sidings and interchange with nearby connections. The busiest was Homan Avenue, just west of Western Avenue Junction, on the Altenheim Branch. That and a smaller yard at 48th Avenue served many sidings on the Altenheim Branch and on the Southwest Branch to Cicero. Forest Hill Yard on the B&OCT main line served the Forest Hill freight station—the largest B&O/B&OCT freight station in Chicago. The facility held 134 cars on 11 tracks and handled most of B&O's Chicago-area LCL traffic. In the 1950s, B&O began handling piggyback trailers at Forest Hill. In Indiana, B&OCT had two yards serving the Calumet District, straddling the state line—the largest industrial district in the Chicago area, with numerous large steel mills, oil refineries, and grain elevators. Whiting Yard, on the Whiting Branch, was the larger of the two, holding almost 1,000 cars while East Chicago Yard, on the main line, held about 350 cars. B&OCT interchanged with two steel-oriented lines—Elgin, Joliet & Eastern and the Chicago Short Line—at Whiting and with electric interurban Chicago South Shore & South Bend at East Chicago. Robey Yard was closed in 1974, with all B&O road trains originating or terminating at Barr Yard. The Robey Street property was eventually sold to C&NW and used for expansion of that road's Global One intermodal terminal.

In 1975, Chessie System began consolidating C&O's Chicago-area operations into B&OCT. C&O trains had used Rockwell Street Yard, a small, congested facility just west of Forest Hill. In 1975, C&O's Michigan freights (three scheduled each way) were shifted to Barr Yard, using B&OCT rails from Pine Junction. The remaining C&O trains—from the Cincinnati line (two scheduled each way)—were moved from Rockwell to Barr in 1979.

Diesel-era BO&CT owned three series of diesels, all Electro-Motive: SW1s 8416–8421, NW2s 9509–9511, and SW9s 9600–9607. All were lettered B&OCT and painted blue. These units were supplemented by B&O Geeps and switchers, which usually outnumbered the B&OCT units. The B&OCT power was largely replaced by Electro-Motive GP15Ts by the mid-1980s.

Straying a bit west of its old home trackage, Western Maryland Electro-Motive SD40 No. 7545 heads a northbound freight across the Great Miami River at Sidney, Ohio, on March 21, 1987. The bridge abutment visible under the center arch was part of the original bridge. *David P. Oroszi*

Continued from page 60

of the bankrupt lines in 1976. During Conrail's planning phase, the prime routes of the former PRR, NYC, and other lines were chosen for its mainline structure. Conrail abandoned thousands of miles of track and received billions of dollars in government subsidies to rebuild the remaining lines. Many parallel lines, such as the Erie across Ohio and Indiana, were abandoned. The resulting system gave Conrail the best routes from Boston, New York, and Philadelphia to Chicago, Pittsburgh, Buffalo, Detroit, Cincinnati, Indianapolis, and St. Louis. Within five years, Conrail began showing a profit, and the company went public in 1987.

B&O's presence in metropolitan New York City drew to a close in 1985 when it sold the remains of its erstwhile Staten Island Rapid Transit to Delaware-Otsego Corporation. SIRT had been B&O's freight gateway to New York Harbor since 1890. New York City bought SIRT's passenger operation in 1971, and the freight portion of the line was renamed the Staten Island Railroad Corporation. B&O still ran a substantial carfloat operation out of St. George as late as the 1970s, but the inclusion of the Reading and Jersey Central in Conrail

eventually crowded B&O out of the New York market in the 1980s.

The demise of the Rock Island in 1980 set the stage for one of B&O's last significant expansions. The Rock's main line along the Illinois River valley served several industries and sand pits which shipped large volumes of silica into Chessie territory. In August 1980, B&O took over service on the former Rock Island between Joliet and Bureau, Illinois, and expanded to Henry, on the Peoria branch, in 1981. B&O eventually signed a 50-year lease of the property, with an option to buy. Beginning in 1982, B&O shared the main line with the Chicago–Des Moines–Council Bluffs Iowa Railroad, replaced in 1984 by Iowa Interstate.

COMING OF THE MEGA-RAILROAD: CSX

The number of railroad companies continued to decline as the industry consolidated into a handful of large systems. By the late 1970s, most Northeastern and central Atlantic railroads had been merged into three major railroads: Conrail, Chessie System, and Norfolk

& Western. Most rail executives saw the reduction of operating costs through larger railroads as the key to survival. With no likely merger partner in the neighborhood, Chessie System began looking south. Chessie System, Inc. negotiated a deal with Seaboard Coast Line Industries and merged with SCL to form CSX Corporation on November 1, 1980. At that time, CSX was a holding company that controlled the railroad companies, which continued their own identities.

SCL Industries controlled a group of several railroads that included the Seaboard Coast Line, Louisville & Nashville, the Clinchfield Railroad, and the Georgia Railroad group. SCL and its affiliated lines referred to themselves as the Family Lines, although the title was never a corporate name. Family Lines served most of the Southeast, so a merger with Chessie would produce a system that covered most of the U.S. east of Mississippi River.

The actual merger of the various CSX railroads and Family Lines took seven years. The first step was taken in 1983 when Family Lines became Seaboard System by merging all the SCL lines into one company; that same year, B&O leased the Western Maryland. The existence of the Seaboard System ended on July 1, 1986, when it was merged into CSX. That left the two remaining Chessie System railroads, the C&O and B&O. The corporate existence of the B&O passed into history on April 30,1987, when it was finally and formally merged into the C&O. The C&O was the last of the CSX predecessor companies to disappear when it merged into CSX on August 31, 1987.

With the merger of 1987, the circle of B&O's history was complete. Over the span of 160 years, B&O had not only fulfilled its commitment to build a railroad from Baltimore to a point on the Ohio River, but went far beyond the requirements of its charter. B&O reached many other major railroad centers— Chicago, St. Louis, Philadelphia, New York, Pittsburgh and Cleveland.

B&O was never as big or as rich as the Pennsylvania or New York Central and went through many times of financial distress. On the other hand, it never filed for bankruptcy and went into receivership only once. And B&O kept its own name 20 years longer than either PRR or NYC. The venture that Phillip Thomas and his partners began in early 1827 had fulfilled its destiny.

To the end of its existence, B&O was always a curious mix of old and new. On July 21, 1984, eastbound train RU98 is picking up some cars at Morristown, Indiana, on the old Cincinnati, Indianapolis & Western—a line that remained signaled with ancient semaphores until 1999. Amtrak currently uses a portion of the old CI&W, from Hamilton, Ohio, to Indianapolis. *David P. Oroszi*

The B&O/C&O merger prompted a major consolidation of facilities in Cincinnati—a particularly important city for both carriers. The result was Queensgate Yard, opened in 1981. The huge new complex was built on the site of a series of smaller B&O yards. Eventually Queensgate (Cincinnati is known as the "Queen City") would also handle trains off former Louisville & Nashville lines following the merger of Chessie System lines and Seaboard System. *David P. Oroszi*

A brochure from the pre-World War II era extolled the virtues of B&O's two pillar passenger trains, the *Capitol Limited* and the *National Limited. Collection of William F. Howes Jr.*

CHAPTER 5

Riding the Capitol Route

PASSENGER TRAINS OF THE BALTIMORE & OHIO

When the Baltimore & Ohio completed its first mile and a half of track in January 1830, it sold—for 9 cents—one-way tickets for a ride to the end of track. Thus began 141 years of B&O passenger service. Among B&O's many "firsts" was that it was the first American railroad to offer scheduled passenger and freight operations. Interestingly, the only year that passenger revenues exceeded freight revenues was 1831, B&O's first full year of operation.

To fully appreciate how far the B&O had advanced rail transport, consider how the railroad constructed its first sections of track. Wrought-iron straps were fastened to stone or timber stringers, and a path for horses was laid between the primitive rails. Top track speed was about 15 mph. The first passenger cars were little more than horse-drawn boxes—with benches for seating—mounted on four wheels. The next generation of passenger equipment was an adaptation of stagecoaches mounted on flanged wheels.

The steam locomotive made its debut in regular service in 1831, affecting every aspect of the railroad from track construction to train operations. Train speeds increased and passenger equipment grew in size. By the mid-1830s, the passenger coach had evolved into a body carried by a pair of four-wheel "trucks" (wheel assemblies). By 1836, the B&O had 46 passenger cars and over 1,000 freight cars. In the meantime a branch had been built from the main line near Baltimore to Washington, giving B&O exclusive access to the capital for the next quarter century.

Track construction was slow and tedious at first. The main line had been completed as far as Harpers Ferry by 1834 and reached Cumberland in 1842. By 1848, B&O's roster included 65 pieces of passenger equipment.

Although some rigid four-wheel coaches were still being used, the majority of cars were of the double-truck (four wheels per truck) variety. By that time freight revenue outpaced passenger revenue by 30 percent.

The very first B&O passenger station in Baltimore was a small depot on Pratt Street. As the railroad pushed westward, business increased beyond the capacity of the Pratt Street facility, and a new terminal was built. Camden Station opened in 1857 to serve both as the Baltimore passenger terminal and the company's headquarters. As the new Millennium approached more than 142 years later, Camden still was serving passenger trains.

RIDING TO THE RIVER

When the railroad reached Wheeling, Virginia, on the Ohio River in 1853, B&O patrons continuing their journeys west from Wheeling had a choice of transferring to a riverboat or crossing the river and boarding a train of the Central Ohio Railroad. The CO provided a connection to Ohio's capital, Columbus.

As B&O was finishing its line to Wheeling, the Northwestern Virginia Railroad was slowly building its railroad westward from the B&O at Grafton to the Ohio River at Parkersburg, Virginia. By the time the NV opened in 1857, it had been leased by the B&O, thus providing B&O patrons with another option to the Ohio River and points west—eventually St. Louis.

The Marietta & Cincinnati Railroad stretched across southern Ohio between its namesake cities, and it made a good connection for the B&O at Parkersburg. At Cincinnati, the M&C connected with the Ohio & Mississippi running west across southern Indiana and Illinois to the Mississippi River and St. Louis. Although the B&O and M&C were standard-gauge roads, the O&M was a broad-gauge line and could not exchange cars with the M&C at Cincinnati. In spite of the gauge difference, the three lines formed an alliance in 1857 to offer coordinated passenger service between Baltimore and St. Louis. Through cars between Baltimore and Cincinnati were ferried across the Ohio River at Parkersburg, but at Cincinnati, passengers had to change depots to connect with the O&M. Although it was a cumbersome arrangement, it gave B&O an all-rail route to St. Louis. More important to B&O's expansion were the two bridges built across the Ohio River in 1871. Those structures allowed passengers to ride the B&O from Baltimore to Cincinnati and Columbus without transfer. Three years after the bridges were built, the B&O reached Chicago with a roundabout route via Wheeling and Newark, Ohio. As the B&O extended westward, B&O President John Garrett was also looking toward New York City.

THE ROYAL BLUE LINE

John Garrett's last major accomplishment as president would be the construction of the so-called Royal Blue Line whose rather complex formation is covered in Chapter 2. As a passenger route, the Royal Blue Line opened for business in 1886, but B&O owned only the 95 miles between Baltimore and Philadelphia, where the railroad built its new depot at Chestnut Street. East of Philadelphia to Jersey City, B&O passenger trains operated over the Philadelphia & Reading and Central Railroad of New Jersey to Jersey City under a joint traffic agreement that created a three-way partnership. Locomotives and crews of the Reading and CNJ moved B&O trains over their respective segments of the route. The opening of the New York extension thus made Philadelphia the easternmost terminus of the B&O, physically but not in operation.

The new route was engineered and built to high standards, and to signify the prestige of its newest (and most expensive addition), B&O in the early 1890s began advertising its New York–Washington service as the Royal Blue Line. The name was derived from the dark shade of blue paint that was applied to the passenger equipment assigned to the New York–Washington corridor.

The Royal Blue Line was unique in several respects. Built as a high-speed passenger thoroughfare, it was the only B&O subdivision to feature track pans that allowed steam locomotives to scoop water while moving at speed. In contrast to the rapid pace that passengers rode over the B&O, though, they had to ride a boat

An early B&O passenger train in the charge of a shiny, trim 4-4-0 calls at Woodstock, Maryland, on the Old Main Line between Baltimore and Point of Rocks, Maryland, about 1885. *Collection of Herbert H. Harwood Jr.*

twice during a New York–Washington journey. At Baltimore, the New York extension initially had no physical connection to the rest of the B&O, necessitating the transfer of entire trains across Baltimore Harbor on a ferry. In addition—and like all the other railroads approaching New York City from the south or west—B&O ferried passengers between its railhead in New Jersey and Manhattan across the Hudson River.

In the early 1890s, the new Baltimore Belt Railroad and its Howard Street Tunnel closed the gap between the Royal Blue Line and the main line that ran southward from Camden Station to Washington and to Cumberland. B&O's second Baltimore passenger depot, Mount Royal Station, was built at the north end of the Howard Street Tunnel; Camden was near the south portal. Mount Royal permitted through train operation whereas Camden Station was and remains stub-ended. Yet, the Baltimore Belt tied in with the old main line close enough to Camden Station such that it could also serve as a stop on the new route to New York thanks to through-service passenger platforms built on the belt line at the junction with the tracks leading into Camden. The completion of the Baltimore Belt eliminated one boat ride for the B&O and made it a better player in the Washington–New York market.

THE CAPITOL ROUTE ENTERS THE 20TH CENTURY

During the 1890s, B&O was redefining its two primary passenger routes: Jersey City to St. Louis and Jersey City to Chicago. As outlined in Chapter 2, the Chicago route was redirected through Pittsburgh and Akron while a true through route to St. Louis was gained when B&O took over the Ohio & Mississippi west of Cincinnati.

When he assumed the presidency in 1901, Leonor Loree embarked on a program to speed up the movement of traffic over the B&O. Many bridges and many miles of main-line track were rebuilt to handle larger and heavier locomotives that could move longer trains at higher speeds. B&O put forth its best efforts to compete with the Pennsylvania and New York Central for passengers between the East Coast and Chicago and St. Louis, but its roundabout route via Washington and its rugged course through the Alleghenies put it at a clear disadvantage.

In 1903 work began on a new passenger terminal at Washington. B&O and PRR were both half-owners in Washington Union Station, which opened in 1907 and replaced B&O's depot dating from 1851. In contrast to its new Washington station, B&O's passenger facilities at New York were far from ideal. B&O trains terminated at Jersey Central's terminal at Jersey City, and passengers had to ride CNJ ferries across the Hudson to reach Manhattan. Rival Pennsylvania Railroad had a similar arrangement but took a great leap forward when it dug a pair of tunnels under the Hudson River to reach a new terminal in Manhattan—Pennsylvania Station—which opened in 1910. B&O tried to make the best of circumstances by advising its travelers that New York's magnificent skyline could be admired from a ferry crossing the Hudson River and not from a tunnel beneath the river.

Daniel Willard became B&O's president in 1910 when the railroad was being confronted with new forms of competition. The onset of the twentieth century had heralded the dawn of the automobile age. The first passenger operations to be affected were local services, but as autos became more affordable and roads improved, the number of riders on longer-distance trains also began to decline. Nonetheless, B&O continued to upgrade its passenger fleet. In 1910, B&O fielded almost 1,200 pieces of passenger equipment. Featuring full-width vestibules, the first all-steel passenger cars arrived in 1911.

UNCLE SAM TAKES THE THROTTLE

When World War I began in 1914, the U.S. was officially neutral but was sending supplies and equipment to the Allies. Rail traffic throughout the country increased sharply as the U.S. became more involved in the conflict, and the nation's railroads struggled to keep trains moving. By the time America declared war in April 1917, the railroads were clogged with traffic. Stations, rail yards, and seaside docks were jammed with passengers and cargo. Under the auspices of the United States Railroad Administration, the government took over operation of the railroads in December 1917 in an attempt to untangle the mess.

Although this period of government control of the railroads is generally regarded as a failure, travelers riding the B&O to New York actually benefited. PRR's New York–Washington corridor had always been busier than B&O's parallel Royal Blue Line, but even the mighty Pennsylvania was overwhelmed by the extra traffic. To relieve some of the Pennsy's

The premier passenger trains of the B&O were the New York–Washington–Chicago *Capitol Limited* and the New York–Washington–St. Louis *National Limited,* both introduced as all-Pullman runs in the mid-1920s. B&O spared no expense in promoting the trains with stylish brochures such as these issued circa 1930. The *Capitol Limited* still operates under Amtrak, but the *National Limited* vanished in the 1960s. Collection of William F. Howes Jr.

burden, the USRA allowed B&O passenger trains operate into Pennsylvania Station in an effort to sway some New York–Washington patrons over to the B&O. In this arrangement, B&O passenger trains continued to use the Reading east of Philadelphia, but at Manville, New Jersey, were rerouted onto the Lehigh Valley Railroad to reach the PRR Washington–New York main line at Hunter, near Newark. The first B&O train arrived at Pennsylvania Station in April 1918. B&O trains were handled by Reading locomotives between Philadelphia and Manhattan Transfer where a Pennsylvania electric locomotive forwarded the train into Manhattan.

THE 1920S: ELEGANCE RIDES THE B&O

Government control of the railroads ended on March 1, 1920, but Daniel Willard managed to secure a five-year agreement with the PRR permitting B&O trains to continue using Pennsylvania Station. Although he was able to get a one-year extension of the deal in 1925, the B&O was finally evicted from Pennsylvania

Station on September 1, 1926. To maintain its presence in the New York passenger market, the B&O was forced to revive the previous RDG-CNJ routing to Jersey City, complete with ferry transfer across the Hudson River. Under the terms of the renewed trackage rights agreement, B&O would handle its passenger trains with its own locomotives and crews over the entire Washington–Jersey City route including the Reading and Jersey Central.

Willard was fully aware his railroad could not match the frequency and speed of the Pennsylvania Railroad between New York and Washington. Instead he decided to offer B&O passengers something the PRR couldn't (or wouldn't): personalized service. The B&O put into service a fleet of motorcoaches that rode the ferries across the river and then shuttled passengers to B&O's downtown ticket office at 42nd Street near Grand Central Terminal. The busses also stopped at important hotels along the way, eliminating the need for patrons to partake of taxi or subways—a definite advantage over the PRR.

In the same spirit, B&O inaugurated a pair of all-Pullman passenger trains in the mid-1920s that were to be the crown jewels of the B&O passenger system. The first to enter service was the *Capitol Limited* on May 12, 1923, followed by the *National Limited* on April 26, 1925. The two trains became the pillars upon which B&O would build its entire passenger network for the next 50 years. The *Capitol* served as B&O's premier passenger train between New York (Jersey City) and Chicago. The equally prestigious *National Limited* operated between New York and St. Louis by way of Cincinnati. Although the B&O was token competition for PRR and NYC in the New York–Chicago and New York–St. Louis markets, it did best by marketing service between Baltimore/Washington and the Midwest.

B&O offered a level of service and luxury that was comparable to or above that of other lines. Courtesy and attention to the traveler's needs was the hallmark of all B&O passenger trains, not just the *Capitol Limited* or *National Limited*. For Baltimore and Washington passengers, the B&O provided a more direct route to Pittsburgh and Cincinnati than did PRR and offered generous meals in its dining cars, making it the preferred choice of business and government passengers.

The 1920s was a good decade for the B&O in terms of revenue, even though more Americans were driving their cars when they traveled on shorter trips. A good portion of B&O passengers were day coach riders and were the most likely to decide to drive instead of ride the train. In the last years of the decade the long-distance market was still strong, but the number of coach passengers was falling and along with it passenger revenues. The stock-market crash of 1929 threw the nation's economy into a tailspin and passenger revenues fell at an accelerated pace. For the next ten years, the B&O struggled to avoid financial ruin, but at the same time introduced new trains and services to attract more passengers.

DEPRESSION DAYS

B&O's mainline flagship passenger trains received the most publicity, but early in the century the railroad operated a vast network of local trains. Many of these services operated over secondary main lines and branch lines and were the most vulnerable to automobiles and busses—and the Great Depression, which severely cut into discretionary travel. B&O tried self-propelled motorcars on some branches in an effort to cut operating expenses, but in other cases the railroad applied to the Interstate Commerce Commission for permission to discontinue those local services that were losing the most money.

There were some bright spots during the Depression. In 1933 the stunning new Cincinnati Union Terminal opened, replacing Central Union Station which B&O had used since 1883. The new CUT was jointly owned by B&O, Chesapeake & Ohio, Louisville & Nashville, New York Central, Norfolk & Western, Pennsylvania, and the Southern Railway.

Changes on the Chicago route in 1934 shortened the running times of east–west through trains. That year, trackage rights were negotiated to reroute B&O passenger trains over 58 miles of the Pittsburgh & Lake Erie Railroad between McKeesport and New Castle, Pennsylvania, via Pittsburgh. The P&LE was a better route than the rugged terrain of B&O's old Pittsburgh & Western, and it eliminated reverse moves for East Coast–Chicago trains in reaching B&O' stub-end depot in downtown Pittsburgh. In the new arrangement, B&O through trains called at P&LE's ornate depot across the Monongahela River from downtown Pittsburgh. B&O trains to Buffalo and Wheeling as well as local trains continued to use the B&O depot in the Steel City.

In 1935, the Pennsylvania Railroad completed the electrification of its New York–Philadelphia–Washington route. The debt-laden B&O could hardly afford to match the feat but wanted to do something to garner public attention—and did so by focusing on rolling stock and on-board services. One of the first and most notable accomplishments in this realm had been the introduction of air-conditioning to passenger cars. B&O had become the first railroad to do this, in 1930, when dining car *Martha Washington* was so equipped. B&O was also an early proponent of a new movement ushered in in 1934 by the Union Pacific and Burlington—the first two railroads to launch "streamliners." Even as the nation's railroads trudged through the Depression, many joined the movement to introduce streamlined trains.

The elegant side of 1920s-era train travel is aptly portrayed in this interior view of one of B&O's "Colonial"-style diners assigned to the *National Limited*. Interior appointments represented the form of Georgian decoration found in early American homes. *B&O photo, collection of William F. Howes Jr.*

B&O attempted to turn the principal liability of its Royal Blue Route—a lack of direct entrance into Manhattan—into an asset after the PRR opened Pennsylvania Station in 1910 by offering trainside motorcoach connections. At Jersey City, passengers detraining from B&O trains boarded B&O-owned buses that were ferried across the Hudson River to Manhattan. Once in the city, the buses circulated passengers over different routes to various Manhattan destinations (one bus even served Brooklyn) including B&O city ticket offices and selected hotels. This handsome brochure from 1940 provided a detailed map of the routes and drop-off locations. Though well-thought out and convenient, the bus arrangement wasn't enough to save the B&O from pulling out of Manhattan and Jersey City in 1958. *Collection of William F. Howes Jr.*

In spite of its precarious financial situation, B&O was able to get a loan from the U.S. Reconstruction Finance Corporation to buy two new lightweight streamlined trains. Built by American Car & Foundry in 1935, the two trains were basically identical but constructed of different materials—one was of aluminum and the other of Cor-Ten steel—for the purpose of comparison. Three new locomotives powered the new trains—two semi-streamlined steam locomotives and a third locomotive that featured a new form of propulsion, diesel-electric. The first locomotive, No. 1, had a 4-4-4 wheel arrangement and carried the name *Lady Baltimore* while the other locomotive, No. 2, was a 4-6-4 type named *Lord Balti-*

more. The third locomotive, No. 50 (no name), was an 1,800-hp diesel-electric road locomotive—the first independent road passenger diesel built by General Motors' Electro-Motive Corporation. (Previous over-the-road diesel applications had been in trainsets in which the power car was integral to the rest of the train.) The 50 gave B&O (and Electro-Motive) an opportunity to compare diesel power against state-of-the-art steam locomotives.

The Cor-Ten steel train was named the *Abraham Lincoln* and placed in Chicago–St. Louis service on B&O subsidiary Alton Railroad. The aluminum alloy train inherited the *Royal Blue* moniker and went to work between Jersey City and Washington. B&O apparently was less than enthusiastic overall about the new equipment and in 1937 sent the *Royal Blue* trainset west to join its mate on the Alton. It became the *Abraham Lincoln* while the original *Abe Lincoln* set was reassigned to become the Chicago–St. Louis *Ann Rutledge*.

STREAMLINED HEAVY METAL

Daniel Willard was still a firm believer in the heavyweight passenger car. B&O still didn't have enough money to make a large investment in new equipment following its brief fling with new streamliner rolling stock, so the railroad decided to upgrade its existing heavyweight passenger trains by rebuilding and modernizing the equipment. To fill the void left by the departed ACF *Royal Blue* trainset, industrial designer Otto Kuhler was hired to design an "Improved *Royal Blue*," and B&O's Mount Clare Shops in Baltimore performed the conversion work on selected heavyweight cars. The new train received a blue, gray, and gold paint scheme that, over the years, would become closely identified with the B&O.

The improved *Royal Blue* was a success, and more trains were converted to streamliners. The next train to get the treatment was the Jersey City–Washington *Columbian*, followed by the pride of the B&O, the *Capitol Limited* and the *National Limited*. While many other railroads were purchasing new lightweight passenger equipment, frugal B&O was rebuilding its older cars to serve as modern semi-streamlined trains.

But, if Daniel Willard's ideas about passenger cars were orthodox, his tastes in passenger locomotives were changing. B&O's Electro-Motive box-cab diesel No. 50 had convinced

management that the diesel could be a viable alternative to the steam locomotive, at least in passenger service. The railroad's mechanical department had been developing steam locomotives equipped with water-tube boilers but was also interested in the new types of diesel locomotives that were beginning to appear.

The engineering staff at Electro-Motive evaluated the performance of B&O box-cab No. 50 and two identical demonstrator units, EMC numbers 511 and 512. With the experience gained from these three pioneer locomotives, EMC designed a new series of passenger diesels designated model type EA (with crew cab) and EB (booster, no cab). The new 1,800-hp locomotives featured streamlined carbodies, each housing a pair of 900-hp power plants and riding on two six-wheel trucks. B&O bought six EA/EB sets to dieselize the *Capitol Limited*, the *National Limited*, the *Columbian*, and the *Royal Blue*, thus becoming the first Eastern road to introduce streamlined diesels on its passenger trains.

Not all of B&O's new streamliners necessarily operated with diesels, however. In 1937, the railroad teamed with industrial designer Otto Kuhler to create a streamlined 4-6-2. Sheet-metal shrouding was applied to Pacific 5304 to produce a rakish, bullet-nosed locomotive that was assigned to *Royal Blue* service. The super-streamlined locomotive even inspired the manufacturers of American Flyer toy trains to offer models of the locomotive. B&O would streamline additional steam locomotives after World War II.

In 1940 B&O purchased 15 more diesel passenger units of an improved design from Electro-Motive Division that allowed it to dieselize even more passenger runs. Similar in appearance to the EA/EB models, the E6-series locomotives served B&O until the late 1960s.

MAINLINE TO VICTORY

Daniel Willard had kept the B&O out of bankruptcy during the Depression and managed to make many improvements to the railroad's passenger services. A few months after his 80th birthday in January 1941, Willard stepped down as B&O's president. By then Europe was at war and the U.S. shuddered at the brink of involvement. When Japan attacked Pearl Harbor in December 1941, rail

B&O's first streamlined passenger diesels were the EA/EB models purchased from General Motors' Electro-Motive Corporation in 1936–37. In this 1940 scene, EA 56 and a booster unit handle a passenger train through Washington, D. C. *Collection of Herbert H. Harwood Jr.*

traffic had already been on the rise for several months. With the declaration of war by the U.S., the nation's railroads once again faced unprecedented traffic demands.

The harbors of New York, Philadelphia, and Baltimore were the busiest on the East Coast and the B&O carried many troops from Chicago, St. Louis, the lower Great Lakes and the Ohio Valley to these ports of embarkation. The movement of military personnel took priority over public travel, but the B&O made every effort to accommodate its civilian passengers with the same high standard of courtesy and service. As one of the few railroads serving the nation's capital, B&O often hosted special trains carrying dignitaries and government officials. When President Roosevelt would travel to his retreat at Hyde Park, New York, he preferred to take the B&O from Washington. His special train would follow the B&O-Reading-CNJ route to NYC's West Shore Route in Jersey City, thence to Hyde Park.

The surge of wartime traffic pushed the B&O's passenger services to capacity as the

tide of the war turned in favor of the Allies. Victory in Europe was achieved on May 7, 1945, but the war continued in the Pacific until Japan's surrender on September 2. Like its fellow companies, B&O's physical plant had been pushed beyond duress, even after the war concluded. Homecoming troops clogged the nation's passenger trains through 1945 and well into 1946.

THE POSTWAR YEARS

At the start of the postwar period, the B&O fielded an impressive passenger-train fleet. In the New York–Washington–Chicago market, the premier train was still the all-Pullman *Capitol Limited*, with the all-coach *Columbian* offering accommodations to economy-minded passengers; both trains operated on an overnight schedule between the East Coast and Chicago, sometimes only a few minutes apart. The *Shenandoah* provided service along the route at later times in both directions. The two long-distance workhorse trains on the route were the *Chicago Express* (westbound)

After the line was built between Baltimore and Philadelphia, B&O began advertising its new Washington–New York service as the Royal Blue Line in the early 1890s. Pacific No. 5304 races through Glen Moore, New Jersey, with the newly streamlined *Royal Blue* in 1937. The streamlined shrouding for this Pacific locomotive was designed by Otto Kuhler and applied in 1937. *W. R. Osborne*

Although trains like the *Capitol Limited* seemed to always receive the spotlight, B&O's passenger network hosted a number of secondary runs such as this overnight local arriving at Cincinnati from St. Louis early in the 1950s behind a polished 4-6-2. *Alvin Schultze*

Shiny new Electro-Motive F3s equipped for passenger service (high-speed gearing and steam generators for train climate control) are ready to roll forth from Grand Central Station, Chicago, with the *Capitol Limited* in September 1947. At this time, the "Cap" was still largely comprised of modernized heavyweight cars. Some lightweight sleeping cars delivered before and during the war were assigned to *Capitol Limited* service, and another batch of new lightweight sleepers would be delivered in 1948. *Collection of Louis A. Marre*

The streamlined *Cincinnatian* made its debut on January 19, 1947, but shortly thereafter the railroad concluded that its intended market—people wanting classy day service between Washington and Cincinnati—did not deliver, perhaps because of the lack of significant population centers on B&O's route between the two cities. The two *Cincinnatian* trainsets were thus reassigned to Cincinnati–Detroit service. Near Dayton, Ohio, on October 2, 1953, the northbound *Cincinnatian* glides along the Great Miami River. *Richard D. Acton Sr.*

The *Cincinnatian* was the last B&O train to be entirely reequipped with heavyweight streamlined equipment that had been rebuilt by the railroad. In this 1961 scene at Lima, Ohio, the northbound *Cincinnatian* still has the original modernized cars, but by the mid-1960s the trains would be carrying a mix of equipment from not only B&O's passenger-car roster, but that of C&O. *Alvin Schultze*

Rebuilt B&O E6A No. 62 leads the westbound *National Limited* out of Cincinnati Union Terminal in the early morning hours of September 2,1956. B&O's regal blue, gray, black, and gold livery helped unify a wide assortment of cars that included new lightweight rolling stock from Pullman-Standard and modernized heavyweight equipment. *William T. Clynes*

and the *Washington Express* (eastbound). They served many localities bypassed by the *Capitol Limited, Columbian,* and *Shenandoah.*

On the New York–Washington–St. Louis route, the *National Limited* continued to be the flagship, with the *Diplomat* providing service at alternate times of day. The *Metropolitan Special* was the route's workhorse train, carrying large amounts of mail and express traffic and making stops at many stations shunned by the *National Limited* and *Diplomat*. Similarly, the *West Virginian* provided overnight local service between Washington and Parkersburg.

Other passenger trains reached cities that weren't located on the B&O's two principal main lines. The *Ambassador* operated between Baltimore and Detroit via Pittsburgh and the Chicago main line as far west as North Baltimore, Ohio, where Detroit-bound trains swung north to reach the Cincinnati–Toledo–Detroit main line. The Cincinnati–Detroit route itself fielded several trains, including a

day run known as the *Great Lakes Limited.*

The *Washingtonian* and the *Cleveland Night Express* covered the Washington–Cleveland route, operating on the B&O west to McKeesport, Pennsylvania, thence on the Pittsburgh & Lake Erie to Youngstown and Erie into Cleveland. Secondary mainline trains also provided service to Wheeling, Columbus, and Louisville.

Daniel Willard's heavyweight streamliners had fulfilled their purpose, but by the end of World War II the rebuilt equipment was showing its age. Like many other roads, the B&O expected to retain much of its wartime traffic and went shopping for new passenger rolling stock. By the mid-1940s the only type of passenger equipment being built was lightweight stock and new B&O president Roy B. White didn't share Willard's disdain for lightweight cars. The B&O placed orders with Chicago-based Pullman-Standard for new streamlined passenger cars and with Electro-Motive for more passenger diesels. Some of the new cars

streamlined heavyweight cars, and lightweight streamlined cars.

By the time the B&O placed orders for new cars, the carbuilders were booked-up for at least a year or more. Anxious to boost its Baltimore-Cincinnati day coach market with a streamliner, B&O decided not to wait for new equipment and instead had Mount Clare Shops create a pair of streamlined trainsets using rebuilt heavyweight equipment. Streamlined from locomotive to observation car, the *Cincinnatian*s made their inaugural runs from each terminal on January 19, 1947, amid much publicity. Oddly, B&O chose steam power for the new streamliner even as it was converting its most important passenger trains to diesel power. Streamlined shrouds were applied to the four class P-7 Pacific-type steam locomotives that would power the new train.

Although B&O would continue to rebuild heavyweight equipment into semi-streamlined stock until 1954, the *Cincinnatian*s were the last trains to be completely converted with rebuilt rolling stock. The *Cincinnatian* never realized its projected passenger revenue on the Baltimore–Cincinnati run, so the equipment (and the name) was reassigned in 1950 to the Cincinnati–Detroit corridor. The run lasted until 1971, although the original *Cincinnatian* equipment had been retired by then.

Only one B&O service would receive entire sets of new lightweight rolling stock at one time: the all-coach *Columbian* received all-new equipment in 1949, including the first—and for many years the only—dome-type cars

were added to existing train consists, and by the late 1940s, most of the B&O's mainline passenger trains were an interesting mix of heavyweight equipment in original form,

Nothing could be finer than dinner in a B&O diner in 1956 as the scenery goes flashing by. This is dinner with the Oroszis—the author's father Paul and sister Karen. Note the Centenary blue china whose famous pattern—which included illustrations of B&O history—was introduced in 1927. Centenary china could be found on B&O diners right up until Amtrak. The decanter in the center of the table held Deer Park spring water. *Joseph Oroszi*

To reduce costs associated with operating local and branchline trains, B&O experimented with—and came to embrace—the Budd Rail Diesel Car ("Budd cars"). Two Budd cars are at the lakefront pier of Cedar Point amusement park in Sandusky, Ohio, in June 1966. B&O began amassing a fleet of RDCs in 1950, using them primarily in suburban-type services but also in intercity service, such as between Washington and Pittsburgh. At least one was used in short-term service between Gary and Garrett, Indiana, and between Cincinnati and Detroit. As this photo depicts, they were also ideal for excursions. This pair of RDCs had been chartered by the Akron Railroad Club and had traveled from Akron to Sandusky via Willard. *Dave Ingles*

During an economization program in the 1960s, B&O/C&O introduced the "Food Bar Coach." In 1966–67 B&O's Mount Clare Shops remodeled five modernized former *National Limited* coaches with 38 coach seats, a compact kitchen with counter, and a dormitory room for the "foodmaster." In this publicity photo which seems to have been sponsored by 7-Up (note the upside-down can of Coke), beehive hairdos are in as otherwise swank passengers go for casual dining in one of the newly done Food Bar Coaches. *B&O, collection of William F. Howes Jr.*

in service on an Eastern railroad. Clearances on Eastern railroads pre-empted the spread of the dome-car concept on most lines, but B&O domes were built to low-clearance specifications. (As it was, passengers could not occupy the domes while trains were operating under catenary on Pennsylvania's electrified trackage in the Washington area.) Not wanting passengers to miss any of the great scenery along its routes, B&O had spotlights installed on dome-car roofs to illuminate the night countryside.

CAPITOL ROUTE CUISINE

One aspect of B&O passenger operations that best reflected the company's pride was its stellar dining-car service. B&O combined fine food and personalized service to make its dining service among the best in the country. The earliest dining arrangements available to B&O patrons were vendors selling food trackside at station stops or during a hectic 20-minute meal break at a depot lunchroom. Dining cars were introduced and by the 1870s had become common on long-distance trains. Gradually they evolved into virtual rolling restaurants that offered some of the finest fare found on any American railroad.

Twentieth century B&O dining-car menus offered fresh seafood from Chesapeake Bay, freshwater fish from the Great Lakes, and a selection of traditional Southern dishes, all served on the B&O's distinctive "Centenerary" blue china after 1927. Generous portions and reasonable prices prompted many passengers to choose B&O trains just for their food.

The dining-car staff usually consisted of two or more cooks and three to five waiters. In addition, during times of heavy travel, one or more "swing" cooks and waiters would be required to handle certain meal periods (such as dinner between Washington and Cumberland on the *Capitol Limited*). The dining-car steward was responsible for the satisfaction of every customer, coordination of the various functions of the staff, and maintaining the car's inventory of supplies. In the early 1940s,

The 1960s ushered in either wholesale passenger train abandonments or consolidations. For example, the Washington–Detroit *Ambassador*, shown northbound at Delray Tower interlocking near Detroit in August 1964, was combined with the *Capitol Limited* (which itself had been combined with the *Columbian*) between Washington and Willard, Ohio. Eventually the *Ambassador* name was quietly dropped, and the Detroit leg of its operation became known as the *Capitol–Detroit*. Hank Goerke

45 stewards, 194 cooks, and 332 waiters staffed B&O's dining-car fleet.

B&O's commissary was located at Baltimore until the mid-1960s when it was moved to Washington. Branches of the commissary were placed at Cincinnati and Chicago to replenish supplies as requested by each car's steward. The B&O maintained this elegant tradition of fine dining on its trains even as deficits from passenger operations rose in the 1950s and 1960s.

THE FINAL DECLINE

The American passenger train began its long decline in the late 1920s as the automobile caught on in a big way. Depression accelerated the decline until the advent of the streamliner in the mid-1930s. Streamliners went a long way in rescuing the passenger train, as did World War II, but after the war the decline resumed—and it continued with avengeance in the 1950s. The automobile became ever more popular in a booming postwar America—a situation further fueled by the advent of the publicly sponsored Interstate Highway system in the mid 1950s. Then, the introduction of jet airliner service in 1958—coupled to a major recession—dealt another blow to the American passenger train.

B&O was not immune to any of these developments, and the effects were initially most critical to the railroad's extensive network of local services. Passenger service on branchlines and secondary main lines required a substantial amount of investment in personnel, facilities, and equipment, but revenues began falling soon after the war as cars and busses claimed much of the railroad's local passenger traffic. The B&O petitioned the public utilities commissions of the states in which it operated for permission to discontinue passenger service on branch after branch, and soon the B&O was becoming a railroad that offered passenger service only on its mainline routes.

The railroad looked for ways to further cut operating costs on its remaining service. In 1950, the B&O acquired a pair of self-propelled Rail Diesel Cars (RDCs) built by the Budd Company that, when run as a single unit, could be operated by a two-man crew—conductor and engineer—thus saving on labor costs. In addition, RDCs could replace short, locomotive-hauled trains and greatly reduce operating expenses. (In actual prac-

tice, B&O usually operated its RDCs in trains of two or more cars, requiring a full crew of engineer, fireman, conductor, and trainman; regardless, the self-propelled cars still saved on operating costs.) The RDCs entered service on B&O's commuter district west of Washington and were so successful that three more RDCs were bought in 1953 to dieselize the Pittsburgh commuter operation. B&O christened its RDCs as *Speedliners* and purchased five more in 1954 for service in the Baltimore–Washington–Brunswick (Maryland) commuter pool.

The *Speedliners* proved their reliability and economy in commuter service and prompted B&O's passenger department to consider Budd cars for longer-distance runs. In 1955 six more RDCs were ordered by the railroad to replace a train comprised of conventional equipment that ran between Baltimore and Pittsburgh. The three-car *Daylight Speedliner* trains entered service on October 28, 1956, and were a hit with the public.

In spite of the success of the *Speedliners* and the public acceptance of streamliners, deficits from passenger operations continued to mount through the 1950s. The grand tradition of the Royal Blue Line passenger service ended on April 26, 1958, when all B&O passenger service east of Baltimore was discontinued. Many other train cancellations followed, as passengers increasingly chose highway or airline travel over rail travel.

THE FINAL BATTLE

By the mid-1960s, the B&O was working hard to stem the passenger decline through innovative marketing techniques. Special fare reductions were offered on off-peak days, meals could be had for less than a dollar in newly remodeled "food-bar coaches," and current-release movies were shown in transit on selected trains. These innovations met with limited success, but not enough to halt the deficits.

In February 1963, the Chesapeake & Ohio took control of the B&O. C&O itself had been fighting a losing battle for its passenger business, but under affiliation C&O/B&O continued to trim losses and yet maintain some semblance of respectable passenger service. C&O/B&O combined duplicative services to reduce costs, and some of B&O's most famous names disappeared. For example, *Columbian* and *Ambassador* operations were integrated into the *Capitol Limited* in the

Despite ongoing losses in the late 1960s, B&O resisted downgrading its passenger service to a status of "miserable," as was the case with railroads like Penn Central. Although some of its once-great trains had indeed evolved to one-coach affairs, B&O at least kept equipment clean, the trains on time, and the service courteous. The *Capitol Limited* in particular was maintained to high service levels right up to the end, offering sleeping cars and quality dining and lounge options. On April 30, 1971, the eastbound *Capitol Limited* heads due west from North Western Terminal at the start of its final eastbound trek to the nation's capital. The next day, Amtrak was the new order of business for most of the nation's intercity passenger trains. *Jim Boyd*

early 1960s. By the end of the decade, B&O's passenger network had been reduced to mainline service on three routes: between Washington and Chicago (with a Detroit section off the *Capitol Limited* at Fostoria, Ohio); between Washington and St. Louis; and between Cincinnati and Detroit.

In 1967, the United States Post Office dealt a blow that would just about be the final proverbial nail in the coffin for the American passenger train when it began cancelling most of the lucrative railroad postal contracts, eliminating another source of revenue for the railroads. All of the nation's railroads were losing great sums of money on their passenger operations by this time. As America's rail passenger network was slowly grinding into total collapse, the government stepped in. An act of Congress created the National Rail Passenger Corporation (Amtrak) to take over what remained of the railroads' intercity passenger operations. As the original Amtrak national system was drawn up, no B&O routes were included.

Amtrak took over on April 30, 1971, and B&O discontinued all of its remaining intercity passenger trains. Commuter service out of Baltimore/Washington and Pittsburgh would the last passenger trains to be operated by the B&O. The Capitol Route's proud tradition of safety, courtesy, and service had come to an end after 141 years.

Five Electro-Motive locomotives led by a former C&O F7 have a freight in tow out of Buffalo, New York, on the former Buffalo, Rochester & Pittsburgh in May 1972. The addition of the BR&P in 1929 provided the B&O access to another Great Lakes port as well as two prominent manufacturing centers, Buffalo and Rochester. *James V. Claflin*

CHAPTER 6

Sentinel Service, Timesavers, and Trailer Jets

BALTIMORE & OHIO FREIGHT OPERATIONS

Baltimore & Ohio's pride may have been anchored in its fine passenger trains, but its freight trains paid the bills. Coal became a B&O trademark early in its history, and the road was a leader in tonnage of that commodity for many years. As its traffic base diversified, B&O competed with the Pennsylvania and New York Central railroads for freight traffic between the East Coast and the Midwest, widening its loadings to include such commodities as iron ore, steel products, grain, and general merchandise.

B&O'S FIRST FREIGHT TRAINS

Train operations on the B&O began in 1830 when those lucky 13 miles of railroad were opened between Baltimore and Ellicotts Mills. Like its first passenger cars, B&O's earliest freight cars were horse-drawn four-wheelers. Flour was an early cargo hauled in large quantities on the B&O, usually in barrels carried on crude flat cars with low sides to keep the barrels from sliding off. The railroad simply referred to these vehicles as "flour cars" although technically they were forerunners of the modern gondola.

When the line reached Frederick in 1831, the horse-drawn runs between Baltimore and Frederick took eight hours, including meal stops and horse change-outs. In 1832, a steam locomotive named the *Atlantic* replaced the horses and became the prototype for a fleet of steam engines—a move which led to the development of larger, eight-wheel passenger and freight cars. As the variety of cargo grew, specialized types of freight equipment were built. Freight traffic surpassed passenger traffic by the mid-1830s. By the 1840s, B&O was designing and building new types of locomotives specifically for freight service. Commodities carried on B&O freight trains now included livestock, iron, tobacco, and stone products.

B&O completed its lines to the Ohio River early in the 1850s, and soon the railroad was interchanging traffic with the Central Ohio Railroad and the Marietta & Cincinnati on the Ohio side of the river. With these new connections to the "West," freight traffic almost doubled from the previous decade. The biggest commodity handled by the B&O during that period was coal. In 1856, 446,000 tons of coal were transported eastward to Baltimore from mines in western Virginia and western Maryland. To handle this traffic, B&O built a fleet of coal cars that resembled a pair of big kettles mounted on a flatcar. The typical B&O coal train of the 1850s was a string of these kettle-like cars pulled by an 0-8-0 "Camelback"-type (cab straddling the boiler) freight locomotive.

During the Civil War, the B&O found itself trying to conduct business on the war's front lines. The railroad suffered much destruction but was eventually rebuilt and returned to service. Traffic levels rose markedly during the war as B&O became a key supply route for the Union Army.

THE EXPANSION YEARS

During the 1860s, eastbound trains operating between Piedmont and Baltimore averaged 25–30 cars; Wheeling to Grafton, 20 cars;

Coal traffic was an important commodity for B&O for nearly its entire life. This photo from about 1870, taken at the B&O depot and hotel at Martinsburg, West Virginia, reveals the unusual kettle-type cars built by the railroad to move coal, in huge chunks, between mines in West Virginia and Baltimore. The coal trains of B&O successor CSX Transportation still move past this building. *Smithsonian Institution collection, courtesy Herbert H. Harwood Jr.*

and Parkersburg to Grafton, 15 cars. Westbound trains consisted of 9 cars from Piedmont to Newburg, and 18-30 cars from Newburg and Grafton. Some of this difference was to balance the distribution and staging of crews and locomotives. Also at this time, trains were operated in convoys. For example, a

"stock special" (livestock train) might run in multiple sections. If a train operated in three sections, the first train would display a placard marked "3," and the last train's placard would be marked "1."

Just before the Civil War, the first marketing of expedited freight service networks appeared

Crewmembers of a B&O freight train comprised of wood freight cars pose with their iron steed at Albion, Indiana, circa 1900. *Collection of William F. Howes Jr.*

in the form of Merchant's Dispatch, operated by the New York Central; Great Western Dispatch, operated by the Erie Railroad; and the Star Union Line, operated by the Pennsylvania Railroad. Not until 1871 did B&O establish the Continental Fast Freight Line, a joint service running over the B&O, Marietta & Cincinnati, and Ohio & Mississippi railroads between Baltimore and St. Louis—the latter becoming a portal for freight (and passenger) traffic to and from the Western frontier.

In the 1870s, B&O reached Pittsburgh and Chicago, creating two new markets for West Virginia coal. At the eastern end of the system, the completion of the Royal Blue Line to New York City with affiliates Reading and Jersey Central in 1886 tapped a huge new market area. B&O's purchase of the Staten Island Rapid Transit in 1889 provided B&O with its own terminal for New York freight operations, although access to the other boroughs of New York (including Manhattan) was by water and the railroad's flotilla of tugs, carfloats, scows, and lighters across New York harbor.

EARLY TWENTIETH CENTURY

By 1900, freight traffic had grown to unprecedented levels. To handle the upsurge, improvements were made early in the new century on 15 divisions of the B&O system during President Loree's term. B&O constructed new freight yards at New Castle, Pittsburgh, and Connellsville, Pennsylvania, and in West Virginia at Keyser and Fairmont. A large locomotive shop was constructed at Glenwood (Pittsburgh). Numerous other improvements, outlined in chapter 3 resulted in a better flow of both passenger and freight traffic.

B&O's heaviest freight locomotives at the time were 2-8-0 Consolidations. Looking for bigger locomotives to move heavy freight trains over steep grades at a faster pace, the B&O in 1904 bought the first Mallet-type locomotive to be constructed for service in North America—the first of many articulated steam locomotives that B&O would obtain over the next 40 years.

During the Daniel Willard years (1910–1941), major improvements were again made to the growing B&O system, and Willard's administration also made important line acquisitions which added new markets to freight and passenger operations. Among the most important was the 1917 purchase of the former Cincinnati, Hamilton & Dayton, giving B&O a direct route between Cincinnati and the

Great Lakes port of Toledo. In later years the Toledo Division, as it became known, grew into an important conduit for iron ore and coal traffic moving between Toledo and Cincinnati.

The 1920s were a decade of prosperity for B&O as it carried record amounts of freight tonnage. At the turn of the century, B&O had made more than three dollars in freight revenues for every dollar of passenger revenue received. By 1920, the margin had widened to 6-to-1. Many new freight locomotives were bought during the 1920s to replace older and slower engines. Thousands of new freight cars were also added, and by 1925 B&O rostered some 99,600 cars.

DEPRESSION AND WAR

B&O continued to expand as it absorbed a number of smaller lines, perhaps the most notable of the Depression era being the 1932 purchase of the 520-mile Buffalo, Rochester & Pittsburgh Railroad and the Buffalo & Susquehanna Railway, a 228-mile carrier. Although B&O envisioned the BR&P and B&S as key links in the creation of a new route between New York and Chicago, that did not materialize. Nonetheless, the BR&P gave B&O access to the industrial cities of Buffalo and Rochester and another port on the Great Lakes.

As more roadways were improved or built during the 1920s, B&O began losing some of its freight business to the fledgling trucking industry. Following the 1929 stockmarket crash, the economy slowed and traffic levels fell nationwide. As with other railroads, the B&O experienced some of its worst times during the Great Depression. Freight revenues in 1935 were $50 million below 1930 levels, while passenger revenues were cut in half.

The wagontop boxcar and caboose were designed to eliminate roof sheets in their construction, simplifying construction while increasing the overall strength of the carbody. For years the wagontop-style of construction was a B&O signature. The first wagontop caboose, car No. C2501, was built in 1935. The C2465, shown here in Hamilton, Ohio in 1965, was one of a group of cabooses built in 1941–42. *Fred Fox photo, collection of David P. Oroszi*

Daniel Willard managed to keep B&O out of bankruptcy by obtaining a series of loans from the federal government's Reconstruction Finance Corporation, but business remained flat through the end of the decade. In spite of financial hard times, B&O's mechanical department created some of the railroad's most interesting pieces of rolling stock during this period. While B&O's passenger department received rebuilt heavyweight streamliners, the freight department received some of the most-distinctive boxcars and cabooses on any American railroad at the time. The "wagontop" boxcar and caboose design eliminated roof sheets in their construction, and for years wagontop cars were a B&O signature.

As World War II unfolded, B&O's traffic increased steadily. When America joined the war at the end of 1941, the nation's railroads were saddled with even more freight and passengers than they had carried during World War I. The carriers were strained to their limits, but unlike World War I, there was no government takeover of the railroads.

German submarine attacks on shipping along America's Atlantic and Gulf coasts forced the transport of petroleum and its products to be shifted to the railroads. Solid trains of oil-filled tank cars were common on the nation's rail arteries until new pipelines could be built.

The construction of new railroad equipment was restricted during the war, but B&O was allowed to rebuild 40 steam locomotives into dual service 4-8-2 Mountain types in its Mount Clare shops. B&O also bought its last new steam locomotives, 30 Class EM-1 2-8-8-4s, in 1944 and 1945. More significant was the delivery of B&O's first diesel freight locomotives in 1942 (chapter 8).

POSTWAR IMPROVEMENTS

After World War II, between January 1946 and July 1949, B&O spent $49 million on improvements to its physical plant. Three new freight yards were built to improve traffic flow. Built at a cost of $2.5 million, Mill Creek Yard opened in Cincinnati to classify northbound coal movements for the Lake Erie docks at Toledo and other northern destinations. Mill Creek was equipped with 16 classification tracks and had a capacity of 1,198 cars. At East St. Louis, Cone Yard—with 39 tracks and a 1,062-car capacity—was built to permit rapid

Triple headed EM-1s stampede through West Farmington, Ohio, with a northbound coal train in September 1956. The train is on B&O's Lake Branch between Youngstown and Fairport, Ohio, the latter a rail-to-water port on Lake Erie. *Herbert H. Harwood Jr.*

classification and delivery of cars to connecting yards in the St. Louis metro area and reduce the time it took to make up trains. Barr Yard was opened in the Chicago suburb of Riverdale to expedite the classification, delivery, and dispatching of cars to customers and connecting roads on the Baltimore & Ohio Chicago Terminal.

Aside from upgrading several of its classification yards, B&O also made improvements to facilities that handled mineral traffic. Some $18 million was spent to construct a coal and ore dock at Toledo whose operation would be shared with rival New York Central. The yard was equipped with three automatic car dumpers and two ore unloading machines, each capable of removing ore from ships at a rate of 15–18 tons per minute. Coal from mines in West Virginia, Ohio, and Kentucky was dumped at Toledo for movement to various Great Lakes and Canadian points.

Farther east, along the shore of Lake Erie, a new coal dock was installed at Lorain, Ohio, to handle coal from the Gauley mine region of West Virginia. This facility had an electrically operated automatic dumper that loaded vessels at a rate of one hopper car per minute. An ore unloading facility was also constructed at Lorain for iron ore being forwarded to the steel-mill districts at Massillon, Canton, and Youngstown, Ohio, and at Pittsburgh and Johnstown, Pennsylvania.

B&O's waterfront facilities and marine operations were likewise upgraded, including the 1949 installation of a new coal-transfer facility at Howland Hook on Staten Island. This dock transferred coal from rail hoppers to barges for shipment to customers on the other side of New York Harbor.

STEEL, MEAT, BANANAS, AND AUTOS

To serve the mill districts of Johnstown, Pittsburgh, and Youngstown, B&O operated trains called *Steel Special*s. The *Johnstown Steel Special* operated between Johnstown and Pittsburgh; the *Western Steel Special* ran west from Pittsburgh; and the *Eastern Steel Special* ran from Pittsburgh to Baltimore. The *Youngstown Steel Special* and *Detroit Steel Special* ran between New Castle and Willard. These trains handled sheet steel for the automotive industry, as well as oil and gas pipe for the petroleum centers of the South Central and Southwestern U.S.

Although livestock traffic is usually closely associated with Western roads, the B&O operated a fairly extensive network of stock traffic, maintaining stock pens at Baltimore, Brunswick, Cumberland, Connellsville, Willard, Newark (Ohio), Cincinnati, and East St. Louis. When 25 or more cars of livestock were to be shipped, B&O would schedule one of its *Stock Special*s. A stock train dispatched from Chicago would stop at Willard for watering and feeding before departing east for Cumberland, the next water and feed stop.

Until the early 1960s, livestock was transported in standard 40-foot, wood-slatted livestock cars. In 1961, B&O placed into service 86 new 50-foot livestock cars referred to as "deluxe livestock Pullmans." These specially designed cars were not only 10 feet longer than conventional cars, but were also higher and wider. The cars were painted aluminum to reflect solar heat and were lettered "Baltimore & Ohio Livestock Special."

Bananas have long been among the most perishable of produce traffic, and B&O handled the tropical fruit through the United Fruit Terminal at Baltimore. From there, the traffic was dispatched on the *Banana Special* operating between Locust Point Yard at Baltimore and Detroit. The train was operated only on days when 25 or more cars could be assembled for shipment.

Auto parts from Michigan and Ohio plants going to assembly plants in Baltimore and Wilmington were another source of freight traffic for the B&O. Auto parts traffic was handled on train No. 396, a fast freight operating between Toledo and Philadelphia. Several other B&O trains also carried auto parts traffic,

A Class Q-3T 2-8-2 is working the Lorain–Medina local freight at Lester, Ohio, in 1956. This was an era when nearly every town had an open depot and an agent to handle freight and passenger traffic. *Herbert H. Harwood Jr.*

such as the *Dixie Automobile Special*, which operated between Toledo's Rossford Yard and Cincinnati, making connections with the Louisville & Nashville and the Southern Railway. The Cincinnati–Toledo route became an important conduit for auto parts traffic as well as for finished vehicles.

COAL TRAFFIC

Coal traffic accounted for 44 percent of all freight tonnage handled by the B&O in 1950. B&O's coal operations were focused on the Monongah Division since 60 percent of the coal handled by B&O originated at mines on this division. Grafton was the heart of the Monongah Division, and three coal branches radiated from Grafton: the Fairmont Subdivision to Fairmont and Wheeling; the Parkersburg Subdivision to Clarksburg and Parkersburg; and the Cowen Subdivision to Cowen. Other branchlines radiated from each of these lines and provided a substantial amount of coal traffic for the railroad.

In 1948, the railroad opened the 8.8-mile Elk Creek Spur, in actuality an extension of the former Berryburg Branch. One mine on the Elk

Creek Spur generated 100 coal cars daily. Between Cowen and Grafton, trains operated at up to 85 cars. Due to the steep grades in the area, trains usually had to "double the hill"—that is, be split into two sections and hauled up the hill one section at a time—before arriving at Grafton.

The Monongah Division consisted of several coal districts. The Northern West Virginia region included mines within a 20-mile radius of Fairmont—the largest and most productive mines on the B&O system. This region also covered the areas down the West Fork River to Lumberport, west of Clarksburg to Wolf Summit, and east to Grafton. The lower part of the region covered the Elkins and Buckhannon areas, including the Elk Subdivision. Heavy coal tonnage—as much as 8 million tons annually—originated in the Gauley-Sewell district.

Grafton was the principal gathering point for coal traffic on the division, so all coal trains originating at mines on the division were funneled through there. From Grafton, trains were dispatched north toward Wheeling and Lorain, westward to Cincinnati, and east

B&O coal operations were centered on the Monongah Division in western West Virginia. Grafton was the focal point, with three major coal branches radiating from there. Four brand-new GP38s near Grafton in November 1967 are about to test their might with hoppers laden with "black diamonds." *Jim Boyd*

toward Cumberland and Eastern destinations. Coal trains operating to Cumberland were called "coal drags" while returning empties were referred to as "coal cars." Trains operating on the Fairmont Subdivision were nicknamed "Fairmonters," while trains destined for Benwooders Yard at Wheeling were called "Benwooders." (It seems that few railroads had as many names—real or colloquial—for freight trains as did the Baltimore & Ohio.)

Coal traffic also came from southwestern Pennsylvania, much of it from the Fairmont, Morgantown & Pittsburgh Subdivision at Connellsville. Other B&O coal-producing regions included southeastern Ohio, with that traffic classified at Holloway, Ohio, and the Buffalo Division's Indiana Subdivision. Coal traffic on the Buffalo Division was centered at Riker Yard in Punxsutawney, Pennsylvania, on the old Buffalo, Rochester & Pittsburgh.

SENTINELS, TIMESAVERS, AND OTHER MANIFESTS

In an effort to boost its carload and less-than-carload (LCL) freight business, B&O developed new programs after the war. On March 3, 1947, the B&O introduced its Sentinel Freight Service. The genesis of this service began the previous year when B&O conducted a survey with its customers, finding many dissatisfied with the handling of their freight shipments. After further research, B&O management concluded that service improvements required the coordination of three factors: the switching of cars from a shipper's siding or a connecting railroad; the schedules of trains handling the cars; and the placement of cars at the destination.

To address the situation, B&O established cut-off times for receiving cars that were synchronized with "symbol" freight-train departures at origin or point of receipt from connections. At destination, latest placement times were established for arriving trains.

The main part of the new Sentinel Service program was the *Blue Book of Sentinel Service*. The book contained vital information for B&O shippers, including a terminal map showing public facilities available, types of facilities such as "team" (public-access) track, automobile platforms, cranes, and such as well as day schedules between Sentinel Service cities. One of the features of the *Blue Book* was the Traffic Plan page, which allowed a carload of freight to be precisely scheduled by B&O. Another key segment of the Sentinel Service program was

the use of automatic records. B&O assigned a group of clerks (called "Sentinels," of course) to the Sentinel Service Bureau at Baltimore. The Sentinels followed the movement of cars and notified both on-line and off-line customers of any interruption of service.

To advertise the new service, B&O painted a fleet of boxcars an attractive silver-and-blue scheme. Car sides were adorned with B&O's slogans for the service: "Siding-to-Siding Dependability" and "Sentinel Fast Freight Service." By 1950, over 32 cities across the B&O system were part of the SX (Sentinel Service) program, providing over 600 origin-to-destination services for shippers and receivers of carload freight.

Another freight service innovation was Timesaver Service. Inaugurated in March 1950, this premium service handled LCL freight between such key points as New York, Philadelphia, Baltimore, Chicago, and St. Louis. One of the chief factors in the efficient operation of B&O's Timesaver Service was the coordination of train scheduling and freighthouse operations, with local pick-up and delivery service available. The LCL shipments moved on dedicated trains called *Timesavers* that operated at passenger-train speeds (*Timesavers* were considered first-class trains), providing second-morning service between the East Coast and the Midwest.

Principal classification points for the new service were at Cumberland, Cincinnati, and Willard. Westbound traffic originating at New York, Philadelphia, and Baltimore was forwarded to Cumberland. There, Chicago traffic was reclassified and dispatched in two sections— the *Advance Chicago Timesaver* and the *Chicago Timesaver*—as was traffic to East St. Louis—the *Advance St. Louis Timesaver* and *St. Louis Timesaver*. Eastbound *Timesaver* trains dispatched from Cumberland were the

A B&O-issued map from 1958 featured a panel of advertising that highlighted the railroad's freight services. *Collection of J. P. Baukus Jr.*

New York Timesaver, Philadelphia Timesaver, and *Baltimore Timesaver.*

Connecting trains were scheduled such that *Timesaver*-type service could be had at selected cities not located on the main *Timesaver* service routes, including Cleveland, Columbus, Dayton, Indianapolis, Louisville, Wheeling, and Huntington, West Virginia. The section from St. Louis made Louisville, Dayton, and Indianapolis connections at Cincinnati while the section from Chicago exchanged traffic for Cleveland and Columbus at Willard.

The backbone of B&O's network of non-mineral freight services were general merchandise trains, which handled manufactured goods. Eastbound general-merchandise freights included the *New Yorker* and *Advance New Yorker, Baltimorean, New Englander, Advance Dixie,* and *Pittsburgher.* Wesbound trains included the *Chicagoan, Westerner, Barr 97, Chicago 97,* and *Chicago 197.* By the late 1970s, two intermodal trains were scheduled in each direction between Baltimore and Chicago. Run-through operations were implemented with trains CW94 and CW97, which operated to and from C&NW's Proviso Yard, picking up and setting off at Barr.

Baltimore & Ohio's Sentinel and *Timesaver* freight programs were both instituted to help the railroad retain its carload and LCL merchandise traffic. But through the 1950s, construction of new highways had allowed the trucking industry to wrest much of this business away from railroads, and new thinking in rail freight transport had to be considered. In the big picture it would be called "intermodal," and it would revolve around the trailer-on-flatcar or "piggyback" format.

TRAILER-ON-FLATCAR

Several railroads were developing a new type of freight service in the early 1950s that offered dock-to-dock service to customers. The concept of carrying truck trailers on flatcars dated from the days of horse-drawn wagons. In the years following World War II, it became apparent to the management of several railroads that trucks offered shippers a range of flexible services that the railroads could not provide. This led to the development of trailer-on-flatcar freight programs on railroads such as Chicago Great Western, New Haven, and Southern Pacific.

B&O implemented its own intermodal service on July 20, 1954. The new program was

Handsome in B&O's intricate tri-tone livery, an A-B-B set of Electro-Motive F3s hustle through Walkerton, Indiana, in 1961 with a westbound freight on the Pittsburgh–Chicago main line. *Dave Ingles*

dubbed TOFCEE (trailer-on-flat-car, with the double "Es" added to prompt correct pronunciation) service and provided 14 key cities between New York and Chicago with piggyback freight service. In the beginning, a total of 185 trailers—both the closed-van and flatbed-type units—were assigned to the service. These first trailers were painted in a blue-and-orange "sunburst" paint scheme. During the 1950s, TOFCEE shipments were handled on *Timesaver* and selected manifest trains.

In 1956, the TOFCEE network was expanded to include the New York City and northern New Jersey area via the Jersey Central railroad. To extend TOFCEE services to St. Louis, B&O began using a detachable trailer body system in March 1960 whereby the trailer wheels could be quickly removed and the trailer body mounted directly on a flatcar. This arrangement allowed the trailers to fit within the tight clearances of the St. Louis route. Specially built cranes were installed at East St. Louis, Philadelphia, and Jersey City, while gantry cranes were modified at Baltimore and Washington to transfer trailer bodies between flatcars and trailer chassis for highway transport.

In July 1960, TOFCEE traffic escalated significantly, and B&O's intermodal department established high-speed, all piggyback freight schedules called *Trailer Jets*. These dedicated trains expedited time-sensitive piggyback traffic across the B&O system on a priority basis, essentially replacing the *Timesaver*s.

The Chicago–New York corridor featured two trains, the *New York Trailer Jet* and the *Chicago Trailer Jet*. The *New York Trailer Jet* operated between Chicago's Robey Street Yard and Jersey City, handling trailers for Washington (including Potomac Yard connections), Baltimore, Philadelphia, and in New Jersey at Elizabethport, Newark, and Jersey City (including Cranford Junction/Staten Island livestock). The train's westbound counterpart, the *Chicago Trailer Jet*, operated between Jersey City and Forest Hill Yard on Chicago's South Side carrying TOFCEE traffic for the whole Chicago area. Both trains operated on a 29-hour schedule between terminals.

On the New York–St. Louis main line, two *Trailer Jet*s were carded. Eastbound service was provided by the *Manhattan Trailer Jet* operating between Lower Yard at East St. Louis and Jersey City. The *St. Louis Trailer Jet* provided westbound service between Jersey City and East St. Louis. These trains were scheduled for a 34-hour run between terminals.

Besides the regular *Trailer Jet*s, certain manifest trains also handled piggyback business, including the *Advance Manhattan, Baltimore Jet, New England 96, Louisville 90, Advance Cincinnatian, Midwesterner, St. Louisan* and *Southwest Steel Special.*

B&O continued to expand its piggyback services, even after the 1963 C&O takeover. To handle truck trailers loaded directly on flatcars on the St. Louis Gateway route, B&O engineering forces eliminated several low clearances in West Virginia between Clarksburg and Parkersburg. Part of the route was relocated and several tunnels were eliminated, allowing the movement of larger freight equipment. This eliminated the need to dismount trailers from highway wheels. Almost immediately, freight traffic doubled over the St. Louis main line.

B&O implemented dedicated intermodal service in 1954, providing 14 cities between the East Coast and Midwest with piggyback freight service. B&O called the new program "TOFCEE," playing on the industry-wide acronym for trailer-on-flat-car service: TOFC. This ad from 1959 illustrates the concept. *Collection of Dave Ori*

By the late 1960s, intermodal traffic had increased enough on the Cumberland–St. Louis main line to warrant additional train service. A *Cincinnati Jet* was established between Cumberland and Cincinnati, operating on a 14-hour schedule and carrying TOFCEE trailers and other selected merchandise, in boxcars, for Cincinnati. Between Cincinnati and East St. Louis, two additional trains were added to the westbound line-up. The *Advance St. Louis Trailer Jet* operated on an eight-hour schedule between Storrs Yard at Cincinnati and Lower Yard at East St. Louis. This train carried intermodal traffic for St. Louis and connecting traffic for the Terminal Railroad Association of St. Louis. An additional train, dubbed simply as the *Second St. Louis Jet*, was established and provided service between Cincinnati and East St. Louis.

The 1970s brought further changes to B&O's intermodal network. In 1976, the *Philadelphia Trailer Train* was established with its counterpart, the *Chicago Trailer Train*. To handle the increase in intermodal traffic on the Chicago–Philadelphia corridor, the *Baltimore Trailer Train* was established in 1981. Operating between Forest Hill Yard at Chicago and Carroll Yard in Baltimore, the *Baltimore Trailer Train* carried intermodal traffic for Washington and Baltimore, including perishables for Brunswick, Maryland. Its counterpart was the

On February 14, 1981, an eastbound piggyback train blasts its way past a pair of B&O's signature color position-light signals at Lodi, Ohio. *Mark Perri*

Baltimore–Chicago Trailer Train. B&O also established two trains to handle intermodal traffic between Toledo and Lima, Ohio, in 1981. The *Toledo–Lima Trailer Train* operated on a four-hour schedule and carried intermodal traffic for Philadelphia and Baltimore that was set out at Fostoria to be picked up by the *Chicago–Philadelphia Trailer Train* and *Baltimore Trailer Train.* Its counterpart was the *Lima Trailer Train.*

By the early 1980s, the railroad was operating three scheduled through freights on the Cumberland–St. Louis main line. The *Philadelphia Trailer Train* operated between East St. Louis and Synder Avenue Yard at Philadelphia on a 40-hour schedule. Its counterpart was the *St. Louis Trailer Train.* A third train, the *Cincinnati Trailer Train*, ran between West Baltimore and the new Queensgate Yard at Cincinnati.

Major revisions were made to B&O's intermodal schedules in August 1985 under CSX when several portions of the St. Louis main line were abandoned between Grafton and Cincinnati, ostensibly to reduce operating costs. The *Philadelphia Trailer Train* and *St. Louis Trailer Train* were abolished and replaced by the *Northeast Trailer Train* and *Southwest Trailer Train.* These trains ran between Wilmington, Delaware, and East St. Louis over a roundabout route that took them over the Chicago main line between Wilmington and Deshler, Ohio, thence south to Cincinnati on the old CH&D and west to St. Louis on the St. Louis main line. This new routing increased transit times to the point that the schedules were no longer competitive, and CSX discontinued the *Philadelphia Trailer Train* and *St. Louis Trailer Train* not long after they were introduced. This left intermodal service only on the Philadelphia–Chicago route.

FREIGHT YARDS

In 1948, B&O maintained 69 freight yards across its system, with main classification yards at Cumberland, Willard, Chicago, and East St. Louis. B&O traffic volume during the 1940s and 1950s was heavy, as over 125 time freights were scheduled daily to move freight over the 6,200-mile system. Highlights of selected yards follow.

Cumberland Yard: Cumberland, junction of the Chicago and St. Louis main lines, was the heart of B&O freight operations. B&O's first yards at Cumberland were located just east of the Queen City Hotel and depot. As traffic grew, the yards were expanded farther east along the main line. The old yard east of the station was used for westbound traffic while eastbound traffic was handled at Virginia Avenue. Classification "humps" were installed in both yards in 1902 so that car sorting could be handled by gravity. Initially, these were "rider humps" requiring brakemen to ride each car off the hump to manually apply brakes. Mechanical car retarders were placed in service in 1947, making the classification of freight traffic much safer, less labor-intensive, cheaper, and faster.

In the late 1940s, the eastbound yard at Cumberland was a busy place. On average about 1,700 cars were humped daily—the equivalent of about 20 trains. Of those 1,700 cars, 400 were coal cars and 1,300 were merchandise freight.

In the 1950s, B&O consolidated much of its Eastern-points classification work at Cumberland. Prior to that, classification was performed at Brunswick and at five different yards around Baltimore. A new westbound yard was constructed north of the eastbound yard and old main line. The new yard consisted of a 10-track receiving yard, which began at M Tower at Mexico Farms, and a 32-track classification yard; total yard capacity was 1,660 cars. The westbound yard was equipped with automatic car retarders and a weigh-in-motion scale.

Willard Yard: Originally named Chicago Junction, the central Ohio town was later renamed for B&O's longest-serving president, Daniel Willard. Due to its strategic location on the western part of the B&O, Willard was a key terminal on the New York–Chicago main line. Westbound, Willard classified traffic for Chicago, Toledo, Lima, Cincinnati, and Cleveland, while eastbound traffic was classified for Pittsburgh, Cumberland, Baltimore, and Philadelphia. In the mid-1950s, almost all freight trains arriving at Willard were reclassified.

Coal and cargo populate B&O's Cumberland Yard and adjacent main line as a general merchandise train resumes its trip eastward on June 27, 1976. Cumberland's strategic location at the junction of the Chicago and St. Louis main lines away from the high-priced real estate surrounding Baltimore and Philadelphia made it the ideal hub of B&O freight operations. *David P. Oroszi*

B&O 9537, an Electro-Motive NW2 switcher, is on duty at Cone Yard, East St. Louis, Illinois, in December 1960. For interchange with Western railroads, St. Louis was second in importance only to Chicago. *Dave Ingles*

On the eastbound leg, B&O operated multiple sections of *Chicago 94* from Chicago, usually arriving at Willard during the morning hours. Also scheduled to arrive in the morning were *Northeast 94* from East St. Louis, *Lima 294* from Lima and *Toledo 394* from Toledo. These trains were normally classified during the daytime and formed the basis for the fleet of 94-series train that departed in the middle to late afternoon hours. These trains included *Pittsburgh 94*, *New York 94*, *Youngstown 94* and *Cleveland 294*.

Another hot train was *Chicago 92*, which arrived late in the day. This train carried livestock and perishable traffic, so it was quickly reworked at Willard and dispatched for Cumberland. The refrigerator cars were re-iced at trackside icing platforms.

Westbound movements through Willard during the 1950s were also heavy. Some of the westbound trains that terminated at Willard were *Chicago 97* from Brunswick, *Willard 97* from New Castle and the *Western Steel Special* from Pittsburgh. Most westbound trains were dispatched from Willard during the late afternoon and evening hours. First *Chicago 97*, known as the "City Section," departed for Robey Street Yard at Chicago with traffic for Santa Fe, Wabash, and Belt Railway of Chica-

go. Second *Chicago 97* ran to Barr Yard at Chicago, handling traffic for Milwaukee Road, Burlington, and Chicago & North Western. Third *Chicago 97*, known as the "Local Section," also ran to Barr Yard, but carried local traffic for set-off at intermediate points in Ohio and Indiana.

Chicago: As the nation's railroad hub, Chicago was particularly important to the B&O, and the railroad's (and subsidiary B&OCT's) freight facilities in "Chicagoland," as the whole metropolitan area is known, were widespread. Not all freights originated or terminated at the same place. Opened in 1948 in the far south suburbs of Chicago, Barr Yard was the primary freight classification facility and was under the jurisdiction of B&OCT, B&O's subsidiary that connected with most other Chicago railroads. B&O's main yard in Chicago proper was at Robey Street, west of the downtown area, while Forest Hill Yard at 75th Street served as an intermodal facility. East Chicago Yard just east of Hammond, Indiana, served as a staging yard for the heavily industrialized northwest corner of that state—an area rife with steel mills, refineries, and other manufacturing.

A look at some Chicago-based operations in the 1950s and 1960s illustrates the varied manner in which B&O funneled freight in and out of the Chicago area. In the 1950s, B&O had seven eastbound scheduled manifests from Chicago. The *Timesaver* handled LCL, forwarder, and piggyback traffic out of Robey Yard and Forest Hill. Three sections of train 94 took traffic from Robey Yard and Barr Yard to Willard for classification. Another train out of Robey, No. 94-99, took cars for Lima and Cincinnati, while trains 92 and 96 took cars destined for points beyond Cumberland. When needed, livestock specials originated at the Union Stock Yards in South Chicago, destined for Cumberland.

Most westbound traffic came to Chicago on sections of train 97. Typically, at least three 97s were received from Willard each day. The first *Chicago 97*, known as the "City Section," went to Robey Yard, with cars for Robey, Homan Avenue, and Cicero. The second section of 97, the Barr Yard section, carried large amounts of traffic for the Burlington, Chicago & North Western, and Milwaukee Road. Third *Chicago 97* also terminated at Barr, and was called the "Local Section," bringing cars from Fostoria, Garrett, and other points on the Pittsburgh main line. *Chicago 197* from Lima brought cars from

Cincinnati. The westbound *Timesaver* brought LCL and forwarder traffic for Forest Hill, and hot traffic for Robey Street.

Cone Yard: Along with Chicago, St. Louis was B&O's other prominent interchange point with its Western connections. Cone Yard served as B&O's freight classification yard at East St. Louis. It handled the make-up and classification of inbound and outbound road trains, as well as delivery of traffic to connecting roads at the St. Louis Gateway.

Lower Yard, which was located west of Cone Yard, was a multi-purpose facility. This yard was converted to a six-track piggyback facility in the mid-1950s. The facility originally was equipped with one permanent ramp and two portable ramps but was later upgraded and equipped with an overhead crane.

B&O interchanged traffic with Western lines such as Missouri Pacific, St. Louis Southwestern (Cotton Belt), St. Louis-San Francisco (Frisco), and Chicago, Burlington & Quincy at St. Louis. B&O also exchanged traffic with many of the other railroads serving St. Louis. It connected directly with some roads and reached others via the terminal railroads, Alton & Southern and Terminal Railroad Association of St. Louis (TRRA).

Baldwin model AS16 No. 6204 putts along with a transfer freight out of East Norwood, Ohio, past St. Bernard in Cincinnati in October 1965. Toting a bright red transfer caboose, the train is en route to B&O's yard complex in Cincinnati, today the site of Queensgate Yard. *Dave Ingles*

Nose to nose, Class L-2 0-8-0 switchers 848 and 867 are at Willard, Ohio, in 1955, three years before the end of steam on the B&O. Both locomotives were built at the railroad's Mount Clare Shops in Baltimore. *Joseph Oroszi*

CHAPTER 7

The Steam Era of Baltimore & Ohio

STEAM LOCOMOTIVES SERVED FOR NEARLY 80 PERCENT OF THE LIFE OF THE B&O

The development of the steam locomotive closely paralleled the history of the Baltimore & Ohio Railroad. From the experimental *Tom Thumb* to the gargantuan EM-1 articulateds, the steam locomotive served the B&O for 128 of B&O's 160 years.

THE FIRST OF MANY

The first track constructed by the B&O was built for trains drawn by horses. The railroad's founders considered using steam power, but there was practically no one in America who had practical experience working with steam technology. Peter Cooper built the well-known *Tom Thumb* in 1830 to prove the feasibility of steam power, but the small four-wheel engine was more of an experiment than a genuine locomotive. *Tom Thumb*'s race with a horse-drawn train is a staple of early American railroad history books, and though the locomotive lost the race, *Tom Thumb* still proved the superiority of steam over animal muscle.

In 1831, B&O sponsored a contest to provide the railroad with its first true locomotive. Phineas Davis won the competition with his four-wheel machine named the *York*, but its performance was less than ideal and it was retired the following year. Undeterred, Davis went on to design another locomotive in 1832 that was more successful. Named the *Atlantic*, the engine was the first of 14 that were nicknamed the "Grasshopper" type—a moniker that reflected the resemblance of the vertically mounted cylinders and connecting rods to the legs of a grasshopper. The Grasshoppers were all four-wheel types with vertical boilers and gear drives that made them ideal for the

early B&O's sharp curves. They were also the first of many steam locomotives to be built by at B&O's Mount Clare shops in Baltimore.

Davis died in an accident in 1835, and B&O's Assistant Master of Machinery, Ross Winans, took charge of locomotive construction. The next type turned out by the Mount Clare shops were a pair of engines called "Crabs." They were similar to the Grasshoppers but had horizontally mounted cylinders. At the same time, B&O acquired eight 4-2-0 type locomotives from William Norris of Philadelphia. These engines were the first to feature a leading or pilot truck that helped guide them on B&O's rugged, primitive track. The first 4-4-0 (American type) locomotives were delivered to the B&O in 1839. This type of engine became B&O's standard passenger power into the next century.

EARLY FREIGHT LOCOMOTIVES

To handle B&O's growing freight business, Ross Winans began developing locomotives designed expressly for freight service. He reasoned that to achieve maximum traction, all of the locomotive's weight should be placed on the driving wheels. The first of these heavy freight engines were called "Muddiggers," and they employed a spur gear drive similar to the Crabs but were much larger engines. Their side rods were connected to cranks attached to the ends of the axles outside the frame. The cranks had a tendency to occasionally hit the ground along the track, hence their peculiar name. Winans built a dozen Muddiggers during 1844–46.

The next development stage of freight locomotives was an 0-8-0 type that employed

The *John Hancock* was a vertical boiler "Grasshopper"-type locomotive built in 1836 by Gillingham & Winas. It is shown on display at the Chicago Railroad Fair in July 1948. *Collection of Louis A. Marre*

LARGER POWER FOR A LARGER RAILROAD

In 1861, B&O had been operating steam locomotives for 30 years and possessed over 230 engines. During the Civil War, many locomotives were destroyed or captured by Confederate forces. Once the railroad was put back in operation, more locomotives were needed to replace those lost in action and to handle the increased traffic of the Federal forces. The B&O bought and built some 4-6-0s (Ten-Wheelers) for passenger service in 1863 and 1865. After the war ended, the railroad built a few 4-4-0s in its shops and purchased several war-surplus locomotives of the same type from the government. B&O also introduced another type of freight engine with an 0-8-0 wheel arrangement and a conventional cab to replace the Camels. These were called "Jersey Greenbacks."

a more conventional direct-drive arrangement. In 1848–49 Baldwin built four of these engines, while the New Castle Manufacturing Company built two more. These locomotives performed well, and B&O rebuilt several Muddiggers into this configuration as well as some brand new engines.

As more 4-4-0s were being delivered for passenger service, the evolution of B&O freight locomotive design continued. In 1848, a new type of engine appeared called the "Camel" and was destined to become B&O's standard heavy freight hauler. To permit a larger firebox and to improve the engineer's field of vision, the locomotive's cab was mounted atop the boiler. Most Camels were 0-8-0 machines built by Ross Winans, who had established his own locomotive works in the early 1840s adjacent to Mount Clare Shops. B&O also had some 4-6-0 Camels constructed by other builders. The B&O eventually fielded over 130 Camels.

With the acquisition of the Central Ohio Railroad in 1866, the B&O began its expansion beyond the Ohio River. Some of the lines of which the B&O took control during the 1870s and 1880s were broad gauge while others were narrow gauge. In most cases, B&O converted the lines to standard gauge soon after they were acquired. As B&O took over lines that were already standard gauge, it inherited a variety of locomotive types built to a variety of specifications. The majority of those locomotives were of three types: 4-4-0s, 4-6-0 s, and 2-6-0s (Moguls).

Many of the engines lived out the rest of their lives on the lines for which they had been built, but others were assimilated into the B&O proper—a situation which called for a standardized classification for the various types of

The Grasshopper locomotives had been the B&O's standard locomotive until the arrival of the first horizontal-boilered engine, the *Lafayette*, in 1837. The *Lafayette* was built by William Norris and is shown on display at the Chicago Railroad Fair in July 1948. *Collection of Louis A. Marre*

steam locomotives on B&O' roster. In 1884 a new classification scheme was implemented that could evolve as new types of steam locomotives were developed. The new classification system—which would be employed until the retirement of the last B&O steam locomotives in 1958—was structured as follows:

Class A:	4-4-2 (Atlantic)
Class B:	4-6-0 (Ten-Wheeler)
Class C:	0-4-0 switcher
Class D:	0-6-0 switcher
Class E:	2-8-0 (Consolidation)
Class F, G, H, I, J:	4-4-0 (American)
Class K:	2-6-0 (Mogul)
Class L:	0-8-0 switcher
Class M:	4-4-0 (American)
Class N:	4-4-4-4 (Duplex)
Class O:	0-6-6-0 (Mallet)
Class P:	4-6-2 (Pacific)
Class Q:	2-8-2 (Mikado)
Class R:	2-4-4 (Forney)
Class S:	2-10-2 (Santa Fe)
Class T:	4-8-2 (Mountain)
Class U:	0-10-0 switcher
Class V:	4-6-4 (Hudson)
Class Y:	2-10-0 (Decapod)

As freight trains grew longer and heavier in the postwar years, more-powerful locomotives were needed to move them. In 1873, the B&O took delivery of its first 2-8-0 Consolidation-type locomotives. Although the Camels put all their weight on their eight driving wheels, which made them hard pulling engines, they did not track well at higher speeds. By putting a two-wheel pony truck in front of the 0-8-0 wheel arrangement, the Consolidation type was created.

STEAM IN THE GILDED AGE

By 1890, B&O had grown into an 1,800-mile system that reached from Philadelphia, Baltimore, and Washington to Chicago and St. Louis. In that year, B&O was operating over 820 steam locomotives. New routes were still being added to the railroad, but B&O's locomotive roster was becoming more standardized. Some older engines were rebuilt in B&O's shops, but many locomotives inherited from subsidiary lines were sold or scrapped.

The 4-4-0 and 4-6-0 types were B&O's preferred power for passenger service well into the next century. With the completion of the Royal Blue Line to Philadelphia, the B&O needed some fast passenger engines to handle the elegant trains that it was running between Washington and Philadelphia. A new class of high-speed 4-4-0, the M-1, was built specifically for these trains, featuring 78-inch drivers.

The E-class Consolidations were the B&O's freight workhorses during this time. Dozens of new Consolidations were built for the railroad during the 1890s, while many older members of the class were converted to 0-8-0 switchers.

In the early days, the B&O relegated switching duties to horses, but steam-locomotive development progressed, older engines such as the Grasshoppers and Crabs were relegated to this service. As the locomotives in mainline service grew in size, they were less suited to this application, so new engines were built specifically for switching.

POWER FOR THE 20TH CENTURY

In the first decade of the new century, development of the steam locomotive was advancing at a rapid pace. As the size of engines increased, so did the need for

As with numerous other railroads, switching duties on the B&O during the steam era were provided by 0-6-0 and 0-8-0 switchers. One of B&O's L-class 0-8-0s, the 1640, is at work at Dayton, Ohio, on June 27, 1956. *Collection of Louis A. Marre*

B&O began employing the 4-6-2 (Pacific) wheel arrangement in 1906 and used Pacifics to power many of its passenger trains until the end of the steam era. Shown at Washington Courthouse, Ohio, in the 1950s, B&O 5320 is a Class P-9 4-6-2 rebuilt from a P-7 in 1928 with a watertube firebox and Caprotti poppet valve gear. During the period when this locomotive was painted in the President livery, it carried the name *President Cleveland*. Alvin Schultze

steaming capacity. This translated into larger fireboxes, and B&O tried different ways to increase the grate area of its locomotives.

Several Consolidations were built with Wooten fireboxes, which were much wider than conventional fireboxes and specifically designed to burn waste anthracite coal. The wider fireboxes made it necessary to move the locomotive's cab forward, so it straddled the boiler at mid-point, creating difficult working conditions for engine crews. Engineers were subjected to extreme heat from the boiler, while firemen had to work with practically no protection from the weather. This type of engine was most commonly known as the "Mother Hubbard" or Camelback, but it is reasonable to assume that their crews had less flattering names for them.

Several Mother Hubbard types were also used on the Staten Island Rapid Transit. As Staten Island's population increased, smoke abatement laws made it necessary for B&O to use cleaner-burning anthracite coal in their engines assigned to the SIRT. Many of the engines assigned to the island were equipped with Wooten fireboxes.

It became obvious that wider fireboxes were not an ideal method for increasing grate area, so the next step was to make fireboxes longer. This required the addition of a two-

wheel trailing truck behind the drive wheels to support the longer firebox, creating yet another wheel arrangement. The first B&O locomotives to be equipped with a trailing truck were delivered in 1900. They were Class A 4-4-2 Atlantic types and were assigned to passenger trains.

Although the Atlantics performed well, the introduction of all-steel passenger cars prompted the design of an even larger passenger engine. By adding a trailing truck to the 4-6-0 wheel arrangement, the 4-6-2 Pacific type was created. B&O's first Pacifics were built by Schenectady Locomotive Works and placed in service in 1906, and were appropriately designated Class P.

As the size of freight cars grew and the length of trains increased, B&O looked for ever larger freight locomotives to move the heavier trains over the steep grades of its main line. One solution was to add a second engine beneath the boiler to increase traction. The front engine was hinged to allow the longer locomotive to negotiate curves. The new type of locomotive was designated a compound articulated type or Mallet, named after French engineer Anatole Mallet.

Many Mallet type locomotives had been built in Europe during the 1880s and 1890s, but B&O became the first North American railroad to use the Mallet design when it purchased a machine with a 0-6-6-0 wheel arrangement in 1904. One locomotive of this wheel arrangement was acquired, originally designated Class O. It was nicknamed "Old Maude" and would be the first of nine different classes of articulated locomotives to be employed by the B&O. The engine would later be redesignated Class DD-1.

MORE NEW FREIGHT TYPES

As B&O rolled into the second decade of the century, two classes of larger freight locomotives were introduced. In an experiment, B&O had Baldwin Locomotive Works enlarge the firebox and add a two-wheel trailing truck to one of its Consolidation-type freight engines in 1911 to create a 2-8-2. Impressed with the results, B&O placed an order with Baldwin the same year for 150 of what became known as the Mikado type. The new type was tagged Class Q on the B&O and would become one of its most prolific freight locomotives.

The next new class of freight power to be introduced on the B&O was the 2-10-2 Santa Fe type. B&O ordered a single engine of this wheel arrangement from Baldwin in 1914. The railroad was pleased with the locomotive's performance and placed an order for 30 more (B&O Class S) that same year. Numbered in the 6000 series, the engines became known as "Big Sixes."

B&O was also developing new designs of articulated locomotives around the same time. In 1911, the boiler on a 2-8-0 was lengthened and another engine added to make a 2-6-8-0 wheel arrangement. The single locomotive, Class KL-1, was converted back to a Consolidation in 1917. Also in 1911, B&O ordered its first group of Mallets from American Locomotive

A time-honored ritual of the steam era—oiling valve gear and other moving parts—is observed at Dayton, Ohio, while Pacific 5313 pauses at the passenger depot in the 1950s. *Alvin Schultze*

The Mikado (2-8-2) was a popular freight locomotive for many carriers, and B&O had more "Mikes" than any other type of steam locomotive. In this scene from May 1955, Mike 4618—a Class Q-4b built in 1923 by Baldwin—is going to assist Mountain No. 5579 in hoisting an eastbound passenger train up the grade out of Grafton, West Virginia. The 5579 is a Class T-3b 4-8-2 built in 1945 by B&O's Mount Clare shops. *Collection of Louis A. Marre*

B&O's Santa Fe types (2-10-2s) were known as "Big Sixes" account of their numbering series—and size. In this scene dating from July 1956 on the CL&W near Piedmont, Ohio, 6187 and mate head up a merchandise freight. The 6187 was a Class S-1a built in 1926 by Lima Locomotive Works. *Collection of Louis A. Marre*

Company (Alco). The 30 new engines were a beefed-up version of B&O's first articulated, "Old Maude," and were built with a 0-8-8-0 wheel arrangement. Originally assigned Class O-1, they later became Class LL-1. The last locomotive of the order was delivered in 1913.

The next group of articulateds was an order for 30 engines placed with Baldwin in 1916. These locomotives were built with two-wheel lead trucks for better tracking, producing the 2-8-8-0. This batch of engines was divided into two groups of equal numbers and were classed EL-1 and EL-2. Baldwin built the next order for 30 nearly identical engines, Class EL-3, in 1917. B&O liked the 2-8-8-0 so much that shop forces added a lead truck to some of the LL-1s, making them EL-4s.

During this decade, B&O added several new accessories to its steam locomotives to

enhance performance. Superheaters were installed in several classes of engines to increase steam temperature and therefore the locomotives' efficiency. One of the more interesting developments in the days before automatic coal stokers was the coal pusher, which resembled the bed of dump truck. The entire coalbunker could be tilted forward to slide the coal toward the fireman.

As the U.S. headed into World War I, B&O would need every locomotive it could find to move the tremendous amounts traffic that would be carried on its trains.

WAR AND PROSPERITY

When the U.S. government took control of the railroads in 1917 under the auspices of the United States Railroad Administration, it developed 12 standardized designs of steam locomotives. B&O received 100 Mikados built to USRA specifications in 1918, 30 USRA light Pacifics in 1919, and 25 USRA 2-8-8-0 Mallets in 1919-20. Control was returned to the railroads in 1920, and the B&O continued to invest in new and larger locomotives. Between 1923 and 1926, 125 more Class S 2-10-2s were delivered. Baldwin built 75 of the "Big Sixes" and Lima Locomotive Works constructed the other 50. B&O also took delivery of 135 2-8-2 "Mikes" from Baldwin between 1920 and 1923. In addition to all the new power, B&O picked up some used articulated locomotives from Seaboard Air Line Railway in 1922. This group of 16 2-8-8-2s was labeled Class EE-1. Pleased with its own 2-8-8-0s, B&O's mechanical department converted the ex-SAL engines to 2-8-8-0s and called them Class EL-6.

During the 1920s, many railroads were acquiring 4-8-2 Mountain-type locomotives, including B&O's two neighbors, the Pennsylvania and the New York Central. This type of locomotive was being put to use in both freight and heavy passenger service. B&O built itself a pair of 4-8-2s (the first members of the T class) in Mount Clare shops using the boilers from two Class S 2-10-2s in 1925–26. Both engines proved their worth, but it would be almost 20 years before B&O would fully embrace the type.

As B&O celebrated its centennial in 1927, Baldwin constructed the railroad's famous President-class Pacifics. Each of the 20 locomotives was named for an American president and was painted olive green with gold lettering and red and gold trim. These locomotives were originally built for and exclusively used on the New York–Washington Royal Blue Line.

Many new designs of steam locomotives were appearing on America's railroads in the 1920s. The four-wheel trailing truck was introduced, allowing ever larger fireboxes. Several railroads adopted the new types of locomotives, but the B&O opted to stay with more conventional designs—but that is not to say that the B&O did not experiment with its own locomotives.

COLONEL EMERSON'S EXPERIMENTAL STEAM

Colonel George H. Emerson was B&O's General Superintendent of Motive Power and Equipment from March 1920 to January 1942. During his tenure, Emerson left an indelible mark on the design and application of B&O locomotives and rolling stock. In 1927, B&O rebuilt a Consolidation and a Mikado with watertube fireboxes at its Mount Clare shops. The watertube firebox was more common in ships and stationary power plants and differed from the conventional locomotive firebox because the boiler water circulated through a series of tubes that were arranged vertically at the sides of the firebox, thus eliminating staybolts and crown sheets. One of the reasons watertube fireboxes were uncommon on steam locomotives was due to the constantly changing steam requirements of locomotives, unlike those of ships and power plants, which tended to remain fairly constant. The version of watertube boiler that Emerson applied to the experimental B&O locomotives was actually

Carrying the name *President Jefferson*, Pacific 5302 is a class P-7 built in 1927 by Baldwin. Each of the 20 locomotives in this class was named for an American president and was painted olive green with gold lettering and red and gold trim. Although originally built for and exclusively used on the New York–Washington Royal Blue Line, they later were repainted blue and could be seen on just about any passenger train. *Dan Finfrock collection*

V-4-class Hudson 5360, shown at Baltimore in 1936, the year of its birth. The class V-3 and V-4 locomotives would be the last watertube 4-6-4s built by B&O, completed in 1935 and 1936, respectively. *Collection of Louis A. Marre*

a hybrid between a true watertube type and the conventional firetube type.

The watertube Mikado was displayed at the Fair of the Iron Horse in 1927 with the side of its firebox removed to display its innards. Both the Mikado and Consolidation ran well, encouraging Emerson to dabble further with the new type of firebox. Mount Clare shops built a Pacific, the *President Cleveland*, in 1928 with a watertube firebox and Caprotti poppet valve gear. Based upon its experience with the three prototype locomotives, B&O decided to order four new locomotives from Baldwin: a

pair of 4-8-2s and a pair of 2-6-6-2 Mallets. Each pair of locomotives would be identical, except that one would be built with a watertube firebox while the other would receive a conventional firebox for the sake of comparison. Baldwin delivered the four engines in 1930. The 4-8-2s were Class T-I and T-2—the former having the watertube firebox—while the 2-6-6-2s were classed KK-1 and KK-2. The KK-1 was rebuilt in 1931 into a 4-4-6-2, Class MK, but reverted back to its original wheel arrangement a few years later.

It is noteworthy that Emerson's development of watertube fireboxes was allowed to continue through the 1930s, even as B&O struggled through the Depression. Mount Clare Shops turned out six more locomotives of three different wheel arrangements, all

The 5600, B&O's unusual 4-4-4-4 (Class N-1) built in 1937 at Mount Clare, was named *George H. Emerson* in honor of its chief designer. The locomotive featured a duplex drive, with one pair of cylinders placed in the normal position and a second pair in a reversed position behind the drivers. The *Emerson* represented the zenith of B&O steam locomotive design and is shown on the *Royal Blue* at Philadelphia. *Collection of Louis A. Marre*

Pacific 5301 was a Class P-7b outshopped in 1927 by Baldwin. In 1946 it was rebuilt into a P-7b, with streamlined shrouding added for its new assignment, the *Cincinnatian*. Slightly weather worn, the locomotive waits in Cincinnati on August 11, 1956, for its next passenger assignment. There won't be many more, unfortunately. *Collection of Louis A. Marre*

equipped with the new type of firebox. The 4-6-4 Hudson type was usually associated with New York Central, but B&O built four of its own between 1933 and 1936. The first Hudson, Class V-1, was a conversion from a P-1 Pacific, but the next 4-6-4 was constructed from the ground up. A semi-streamlined Hudson the *Lord Baltimore*, a Class V-2, was built in 1935 to pull the new lightweight *Royal Blue* streamliner. B&O had built a similar engine in 1934, the *Lady Baltimore*, but with a 4-4-4 wheel arrangement. Two more 4-6-4s, Class V-3 and V-4, would be the last watertube Hudsons built by B&O, completed in 1935 and 1936, respectively. By that time Col. Emerson's engineering staff was designing an entirely new class of locomotive that, as it turned out, would be the last of B&O's experimental steam locomotives.

As steam locomotives grew in size, some designers were concerned about the amount of wear that piston thrusts inflicted upon track structure. Several railroads were using 4-8-4 locomotives on their heaviest and fastest passenger trains, but B&O's biggest passenger engines were 4-6-2 Pacifics that required helper engines to get their trains over the railroad's steepest grades. The conversion of the KK-1 into a 4-4-6-2 mentioned earlier was an attempt to develop a passenger Mallet that could single-handedly move a heavy passenger train over the rough terrain of the Cumberland and Pittsburgh divisions, but articulated locomotives were not well-suited to the high-speed passenger service.

One proposed solution, called the duplex drive, was comprised of two separate groups of drive wheels, each with its own set of cylinders mounted on a rigid frame. Col. Emerson saw potential in the idea, and in 1937 B&O built a rigid-frame locomotive with a 4-4-4-4 wheel arrangement, a watertube firebox, and two sets of cylinders. Named *George H. Emerson* in honor of its chief designer, the locomotive was assigned Class N-1. Its duplex drive featured one pair of cylinders placed in the normal position with a second pair in a reversed position behind the drivers. The *George H. Emerson* represented the zenith of B&O steam locomotive design. It received much publicity when it debuted but was forced to share its limelight with the new streamlined diesel passenger locomotives being delivered at the same time.

WORLD WAR II-STEAM'S GRAND FINALE

Baltimore & Ohio posed the duplex drive steamer next to new Electro-Motive Corporation EA/EB cab-booster unit passenger sets in publicity photographs. The *George H. Emerson* was displayed at the 1939 New York World's Fair and served on the elite trains of the Royal Blue Line. But it was a unique piece of machinery amongst a fleet of standard B&O steam locomotives and new diesels. B&O management recognized the advantages of diesel power and lost interest in further development of the duplex-drive steam locomotive; the *Emerson* was withdrawn from service in 1943. Oddly, the Pennsylvania Railroad's mechanical department found a great deal of merit in the duplex-drive design. PRR built two groups of duplex-drive locomotives—passenger and freight types—but their experience eventually confirmed what B&O already knew.

In the final years of the 1930s, rail traffic began to increase as the country emerged from the Depression. When war in Europe broke out in 1939, steam locomotives on B&O's roster numbered around 2,000. Most of the diesels in service were passenger units while a few were yard switchers. B&O needed new locomotives to handle increased traffic.

During and after World War II, B&O built a series of 40 Class T-3 4-8-2s for dual service. T-3 No. 701, built in 1942, heads up a westbound passenger special at Willard in May 1958. *Alvin Schultze*

During the twilight of B&O steam, Pacific 5224, a Class P-5 4-6-2 built in 1928 by Alco, drifts past North Dayton Tower in Dayton, Ohio, in the mid-1950s as the operator hands up train orders to the crew. *Cliff Comer, collection of David P. Oroszi*

More new passenger diesels were delivered to B&O in 1940 as America was gearing up for war. B&O wanted to buy road freight diesels, but locomotive construction was restricted in 1942. The railroad decided to build its own steam freight locomotives at Mount Clare. Between 1942 and 1946, Mount Clare built 40 Class T-3 Mountains that were designed for dual-service; they performed admirably under the demands of wartime. Mount Clare also completely rebuilt several P-7 Pacifics in 1942, 1946, and 1949 as it awaited production restrictions to be lifted on new diesels.

Still more power was needed to handle B&O's heaviest trains. The government allowed B&O to obtain three four-unit sets of EMD (Electro-Motive Division of General Motors) FT model freight locomotives, and they were put to work on the Cumberland division. The locomotives were quite successful, but B&O couldn't get any more diesels for a while, and the railroad instead decided to buy new steam locomotives. In 1944, B&O was granted permission to acquire 25 new articulated locomotives from Baldwin Locomotive Works—new engines that were, by any mea-

sure, huge. Built on a 2-8-8-4 wheel arrangement, they were assigned Class EM-1 and were the last new steam locomotives to be built for B&O. The EM-1s weighed in at over 310 tons. To put it in perspective, the Grasshopper of 1832 weighed 6^{1}/$_{2}$-tons. The EM-1s became synonymous with B&O modern steam and were assigned to all types of mainline freight service and occasionally passenger runs.

When the war ended, the restrictions on diesel locomotive production were abolished, and most railroads, including B&O, began replacing their steam locomotives with diesels. Some railroads were converting quickly, and many newer steam locomotives were available on the used market at bargain prices. In 1947, B&O acquired a group of 13 4-8-2s from the Boston & Maine and 10 2-6-6-4 articulated locomotives from Seaboard Air Line.

But B&O was also in the process of switching over to diesel power and purchased new passenger and freight units for the road and new switchers to work the yards. Older steam engines were retired while newer types continued to work into the 1950s. The era of B&O steam power came to an end in 1958 when the railroad retired its last steam locomotives.

B&O's EM-class 2-8-8-4 articulateds were legendary and represented the pinnacle of brute steam freight power on the railroad. EM-1 7614, a Baldwin product of 1944, storms through Tippecanoe, Ohio, on the old CL&W, July 20, 1956. *Collection of Louis A. Marre*

Glowing in Chessie System colors that complement a beautiful autumn day in the Appalachians, a quartet of Electro-Motive diesels make a grand sweep through Bradshaw, West Virginia, on October 24, 1982. These are the final years of B&O's diesel era—indeed, the B&O itself. *David Ori*

Electric and Diesel Locomotives of the B&O

AN EARLY USER OF STEAM POWER, B&O LIKEWISE PIONEERED THE USE OF ELECTRIC AND DIESEL LOCOMOTIVES

For most of the Baltimore & Ohio's 160 years of existence, the railroad relied heavily upon steam power to move passengers and freight. Nonetheless, halfway into the railroad's lifetime, at the end of the nineteenth century, there came a need for something other than steam to move trains, and newfound electricity came to the rescue. Then, during B&O's last half century, yet another type of electric-related propulsion—diesel electric—radically transformed the face of the railroad as a whole when diesel propulsion came of age.

ELECTRICITY POWERS THE B&O

The construction of the Baltimore Belt Railroad in the early 1890s required the digging of a long tunnel beneath Howard Street in downtown Baltimore. At 7,340 feet, the tunnel would be B&O's longest and would run eastbound traffic up a 1 percent grade. The expense of ventilating the shaft to permit the operation of steam locomotives in the tunnel was prohibitively high due to stringent city ordinances.

In 1891, there was no practical substitute for the steam locomotive. Early in the project, consideration was given to cable power for Howard Street Tunnel, but the weight and speed requirements for trains quickly rendered such unsuitable. Electric traction was being applied to streetcars, but electric locomotives large enough to pull freight and passenger trains were still on the drawing boards. B&O approached the newly formed General Electric Company in 1892 to construct an electric locomotive that was powerful enough to move passenger and freight trains through

the tunnel. At the time, B&O and GE were starting completely from scratch. GE built its first electric locomotive in 1893 and its second the following year, but neither was big enough to handle Howard Street Tunnel.

As work on the Belt Line neared completion in June 1895, GE delivered the world's first mainline electric locomotive to B&O. Locomotive No. 1 was actually two, semi-permanently coupled four-wheel units that worked as a single locomotive. Weighing in at 96 tons, it could easily pull a 1,600-ton freight train with its steam locomotive through the long tunnel.

Regular electric operation of the Belt Line began in July 1895 and was a complete success; No. 1 fulfilled all design requirements beyond expectations. A second electric locomotive (or "motor") was delivered in November 1895 and the third in May 1896. B&O classed these first electrics as LE-1s. Although it was only four miles long, the Belt Line electrification was the first of many such applications that would be built by other railroads.

B&O had another electric operation in Baltimore that was overshadowed by the mainline electrification. At the same time the Belt Line was put in service, B&O also electrified its switching operation at Fells Point, east of Baltimore's inner harbor. Fells Point was a warehouse district served by street trackage built with very sharp curves. In 1895, B&O strung overhead wire above its tracks at Fells Point and bought a five-ton electric locomotive equipped with a trolley pole to shunt cars around the tight confines of the district. A larger, 10-ton electric locomotive was bought in 1909 to replace the earlier motor.

B&O 18 is a Class OE-4 electric locomotive built in 1927. It spent its life assigned to the Howard Street Tunnel operations in Baltimore. The OE class would be the last electric locomotives purchased by the B&O. *Frank Swengel Collection, Railway & Locomotive Historical Society*

B&O's first diesel was box-cab unit No. 1 (renumbered to 195 in 1940) built jointly by Alco, General Electric, and Ingersoll-Rand in 1925. It was used at B&O's small yard at 26th Street on Manhattan's West Side as shown in this 1955 view. It now resides in a museum. *Collection of Louis A. Marre*

Back on the Belt Line, the early overhead power distribution system was replaced in 1902 with a more reliable third-rail system. The second generation of B&O electric locomotives was the 40-ton LE-2 Class, a group of four boxlike freight motors built by GE in 1903 and a fifth unit built in 1906.

B&O's third and final form of electric locomotive was the Class OE, a four-axle steeple-cab design. The first of these locomotives were two OE-1s, delivered by GE in 1910. Two more motors, classed OE-2, were built in 1912. With the arrival of these larger motors, the three

original electric locomotives were retired in 1912. B&O bought two OE-3 motors in 1923 and two OE-4s in 1927, allowing all the LE-2 freight motors to be retired that year. The OE-4s would be the last electric locomotives bought by the B&O. Daniel Willard thought about electrifying more mainline trackage, but B&O didn't have the money for it. Baltimore & Ohio would have only one more fling with electric traction in the early 1920s.

Staten Island Rapid Transit was both a B&O freight line to New York harbor and a heavily traveled commuter railroad. In 1923, the State

of New York passed the Kaufman Electrification Act, which required railroads to stop using steam locomotives in New York City. At the time, SIRT commuter trains were comprised of wooden coaches pulled by Camelback 4-4-0s or 2-4-4T commuter engines. To comply with the Kaufman Act, B&O electrified the SIRT in 1925 with subway-style cars. Construction of a tunnel between Staten Island and Brooklyn was planned at the time, and it was anticipated that SIRT would connect with New York's subways. The tunnel was never built, but SIRT continued to provide commuter service with its peculiar subway cars until the mid-1970s.

BALTIMORE & OHIO'S FIRST DIESELS

The Kaufman Act affected another B&O operation on the New York waterfront. Baltimore & Ohio had a small yard at 26th Street on Manhattan's West Side, and it needed a new type of locomotive to replace the steam switcher at this location. The first diesel locomotives appeared in the mid-1920s when GE and Ingersoll-Rand collaborated to produce a 300-hp, 60-ton diesel demonstration locomotive in 1924. The demonstrator was tested by several Northeastern railroads including B&O, and later that year the American Locomotive Company (Alco) joined with GE and I-R to build a production locomotive based upon the demonstrator.

The first of the new Alco-GE-IR 60-ton, 300-hp diesel switchers was sold to Central Railroad of New Jersey in 1925. B&O purchased the next Alco-GE-IR switcher later that year for its 26th Street facility in Manhattan. The CNJ and B&O box-cab switchers performed well and labored many years before both units were retired to museums. B&O also bought a small gasoline-engine switcher in 1926, but it would be ten years before B&O would buy another diesel locomotive.

B&O purchased about a dozen gasoline-engine motor cars of various designs during the 1920s for use on branch lines having light patronage. Steam locomotives continued to handle B&O's mainline passenger trains for many years to come. Few people believed that a diesel locomotive could be built that could handle a full-sized passenger consist.

B&O's mechanical department was developing steam passenger locomotives with watertube fireboxes during the 1930s, but the department's boss, Col. George H. Emerson, was also interested in other types of motive power. Chicago, Burlington & Quincy and Union Pacific each put a diesel-powered streamlined passenger train in service in 1934. Both of these trains were permanently coupled articulated (sectional) sets. That same year, B&O ordered a pair of new lightweight passenger trains drawn by independent locomotives. B&O built two steam locomotives for the trains, the 4-4-4 *Lady Baltimore*, and the *Lord Baltimore*, a 4-6-4. Coincidentally, Electro-Motive Corporation was building a pair of over-the-road diesel passenger locomotives in 1935 to demonstrate that diesels were suited for more than just yard switching. A subsidiary of General Motors Corporation, EMC had built several gas-electric motor cars during the 1920s as well as the internal-combustion power cars for CB&Q's and UP's streamlined trains of 1934. When B&O placed the orders for its new lightweight trains, the EMC design staff had been working on a full-fledged road locomotive with enough tractive effort to match a 4-6-4 steam locomotive.

B&O tested the two EMC diesel demonstrators in mid-1935. The railroad's mechanical department was impressed with the pulling power of two locomotives as they handled a passenger train over Sand Patch Grade. In spite of B&O's tight financial situation, an order for one of the 1,800-hp locomotives was placed with EMC. After its delivery in August 1935, No. 50 was assigned to the new *Royal Blue* streamliner between Washington and New York. The locomotive ran reasonably well, but was under-powered for the size of train to which it was assigned, and it also suffered from problems with its trucks at high speed. In 1937, the 50 was transferred to B&O subsidiary Alton Railroad to power the *Abraham*

B&O 50 was the first self-contained diesel passenger locomotive in the U.S., purchased by B&O from Electro-Motive Corporation in 1935. In 1937, the 50 was transferred to B&O subsidiary Alton Railroad to power the *Abraham Lincoln*, one of B&O's new lightweight passenger trains, and was given a slightly streamlined, sloped nose. The unit served between Chicago and St. Louis well into the 1940s before being retired in 1958. Today, minus its sloped nose, it resides at the Museum of Transportation near St. Louis. This photo shows it at Chicago on June 18, 1937. *Collection of Louis A. Marre*

Lincoln, B&O's other lightweight train. The unit served between Chicago and St. Louis well into the 1940s and was retired in 1959. Today the historic locomotive resides at the Museum of Transportation near St. Louis.

By 1937, Daniel Willard was no longer interested in lightweight passenger equipment, but he *was* very interested in cutting operating costs. He recognized the economic advantages of the diesel, but it would have to come from a locomotive larger and more powerful than No. 50. B&O was in the process of rebuilding heavyweight passenger equipment into luxury streamliners and wanted powerful and fast engines for the new trains.

STREAMLINERS ALONG THE POTOMAC

After the two Electro-Motive demonstrator units completed their touring, EMC engineers went back to their drafting boards to improve on an essentially sound idea. They refined the box-cab body style into a streamlined carbody in which the cab was positioned up and back for crew safety. A pair of new three-axle trucks with center idler (non-powered) axles carried the new design, and two 900-hp Winton diesel engines provided the power. A major advantage of the diesel was it could be operated in multiples from one cab. Electro-Motive's new passenger units were offered as an "A-B" set, a cab ("A") unit that controlled the set and a cabless booster ("B") unit.

B&O placed an order for six cab-booster sets in early 1937. EMC identified the engines as models EA and EB (B&O would be the only railroad to order that model), and they were the first of five different models of E-series passenger diesel that B&O would purchase up to 1955.

The EA/EB sets were delivered in a new blue, gray, and black paint scheme with gold lettering and trim designed by Otto Kuhler. This became the standard B&O passenger paint scheme until the early 1960s, when it was changed to solid blue with yellow lettering.

The first sets of the new passenger diesels went to work on the *Capitol Limited* in 1937, and the remainder of the order was assigned to service on the "new" modernized heavyweight *Royal Blue* when Mount Clare Shops delivered the train in 1938. The diesels were tested against B&O's latest steam locomotive, the duplex-drive *George Emerson*. The lower operating costs of the diesel made a convincing argument in its favor, while the unorthodox duplex-drive of the steam engine did nothing to improve its economics.

The E-unit continued to evolve as Electro-Motive introduced its Model 567 diesel engine in 1939, replacing the Winton engines that had been used in each locomotive. EMC constructed several progressive E-series models until the E6 was introduced in late 1939. Though its catalog period was brief—less than three years—the E6 was a popular locomotive. Satisfied with the performance of its EA/EB passenger units, B&O ordered seven E6 cab/booster sets, and when the E6s were delivered between 1940 and 1941, B&O was able to assign diesel power to its most important passenger trains, years ahead of New York Central and Pennsylvania. Coal accounted for a good part of B&O's revenues, but the operating and accounting departments realized that diesel locomotives could outperform steam power for lower cost.

In the pre-World War II years, railroads began to accept diesel power for passenger service, but they had yet to be convinced the diesel was suitable for road freight service. That changed in 1939 when Electro-Motive produced the FT. Like the E-unit, the FT was configured to operate in cab and booster sets. Unlike the E, the FT was designed to haul freight. Each FT unit rode on a pair of two-axle trucks and was powered by a 1,350-hp engine. Electro-Motive tested a set of FT demonstrators, in A-B-B-A formation, sending them on a tour of American railroads during 1939 and 1940 as war brewed in Europe. B&O was one of many railroads to order the FT after testing the demonstrators.

DIESEL WAR HORSES

As the U.S. geared up for the war, the government took control of industrial output. The War Production Board placed restrictions on the construction of new railroad equipment, and new locomotives and cars were allocated to railroads according to their role in the war effort. Since B&O was an important freight carrier (especially coal), it was able to procure three A-B-B-A FT sets in 1942 and another three FT sets the following year.

B&O was also buying diesel switchers. The

diesel had established a beachhead in the freight yard, if not in over-the-road freight service when B&O began buying diesel power. B&O's third diesel locomotive had been a 600-hp EMC SW model switcher, delivered in 1936 between box-cab No. 50 and the EA/EB streamlined passenger diesels. The SW was assigned to the Baltimore & Ohio Chicago Terminal. More switchers arrived in 1940 when Electro-Motive delivered 16 600-hp SW1 switchers, followed by an order of six additional SW1s in 1942. B&O also received an order of nine 1,000-hp NW2 switchers from EMC in late 1940 and in 1943 three more NW2s were built for B&OCT.

During the war, the War Production Board dictated that General Motors' Electro-Motive Division (changed from Corporation in 1941) could build only diesel freight locomotives, while the steam locomotive builders (Alco, Baldwin, and Lima) could build only steam locomotives and diesel switchers (or in the case of Alco, dual-service freight and passenger road diesels).

B&O continued to dieselize its freight yards during the war, buying two Baldwin VO1000

Baldwin S12 switcher 9230 works at New Martinsville, West Virginia, in 1963. Long a highly regarded builder of steam locomotives, Baldwin had considerably less success with its line of diesel locomotives, but B&O bought a number of Baldwin diesels. *Ken Douglas*

B&O tended to keep its small fleet of Fairbanks-Morse switchers and road-switchers in Maryland. The 9717 in this scene at Silver Spring, Maryland, in 1970 is an F-M H12-44. *Harold Buckley Jr.*

yard switchers in 1943—the first Baldwin diesels for B&O, a long-time BLW customer. (Baldwin would also produce B&O's last new steam locomotives, the EM-1 articulateds of 1944 and 1945.) B&O acquired about two dozen more 1,000-hp switchers from Baldwin by the end of the war.

American Locomotive Company was another longtime steam builder that tried its hand at diesels. Alco built several of its 600-hp S1 and 1,000-hp S2 diesel switchers for B&O between 1943 and 1945, with many of the S2 switchers assigned to Staten Island Rapid Transit. In 1943, B&O also took delivery of two small switchers that were built by General Electric, an 65-ton model and an 80-ton type.

After the tide of the war gradually turned in the Allies' favor, restrictions on new rail equipment were eased. B&O took delivery of 18 new Electro-Motive E7 passenger units in 1945 to accelerate the conversion of its passenger services to diesel power. At war's end, B&O had over 130 diesel locomotives on its roster, and all of the railroad's premium passenger trains were diesel-powered. In contrast, Pennsylvania Railroad was receiving its first E7s along with a fleet of duplex-drive 4-4-4-4 steam passenger locomotives. B&O was fortunate to rec-

ognize the advantages of the diesel over steam at such an early date.

CHANGING OF THE GUARD

In the years following World War II, many American railroads began replacing their steam locomotives with diesels. With such writing on the wall, the traditional steam-locomotive builders transformed themselves into diesel builders to stay in business. B&O's own dieselization program was well under way in the late 1940s as it added more diesel switchers and road freight locomotives to its roster.

Alco, Baldwin, EMD, and postwar newcomer Fairbanks-Morse built a variety of switchers for B&O in 1948, all of them 1,000-hp machines. Alco built 25 S2 switchers, Baldwin delivered 25 DS44-1000 yard locomotives, Fairbanks-Morse provided 10 H10-44s, and EMD built 10 NW2s. More road freight diesels went to work in 1948 when EMD delivered 58 F3 A-units. At 1,500 hp, the F3 was a beefed-up version of the 1,350-hp FT.

The pace of B&O's diesel program picked up in 1949 as the railroad took delivery of its first 1,500-hp F7 freight locomotives from EMD. B&O would acquire over 250 F7 cab and booster units over the next few years, and also

The 4136 is an Alco 1,600-hp FA2 road freight cab unit built in 1953. B&O had 38 FA cab units and 21 FB booster units that roamed the system from 1950 until 1967. In March 1967, a few months before retirement, this FA2 and FB2 are leaving Willard for Chicago. *Jim Boyd*

B&O had a total of 74 F3 locomotives built by EMD in 1947–1949. The railroad originally separated them into three groups: passenger units, freight service, and dual-service (passenger and freight) units. Most of them were used as trade-ins on the GP30s in 1962 and the GP35s in 1964. The 4444 and 4445 were 1,500-hp F3As designated as dual-service units and are shown at Cincinnati in 1958. *Jim Edmonston*

119

Baldwin's "Sharknose" diesels were among the more rare diesel types, and B&O was among the few that purchased Sharks new (others, Pennsylvania, New York Central, and Elgin, Joliet & Eastern). Shown at the Grafton engine terminal in the mid-1950s is RF16A set 4220. B&O purchased a total of 19 1,600-hp RF16As and 13 RF16B booster units from Baldwin in 1950–1953, all for freight service. *Jim Edmonston*

purchased smaller batches of road freight diesels from Alco and Baldwin in the early 1950s. Alco built 59 cab and booster versions of its 1,600-hp FA/FB model—Alco's answer to Electro-Motives highly popular F-unit—for B&O between 1950 and 1953. Likewise, Baldwin offered its own version of a 1,600-hp road freight locomotive, the RF16. The unique styling of the RF16 car body resembled a shark so the type was nicknamed "sharknose." B&O assembled a small fleet of 32 RF16 cab and booster units between 1950 and 1953.

Also in 1950, B&O acquired eight of Electro-Motive's new E8 model passenger diesel, followed by another eight E8s in 1953. On a related note, the railroad also rebuilt 11 of its

One of B&O's more obscure and unremarked diesels was this diesel tractor—complete with standard railroad-issued couplers—used to switch the Fells Point industrial complex at Baltimore. Much of the trackage negotiated the cobblestone streets with tight-radius curves and switches. Using a tractor obviated the need for runaround tracks to change from one car end to another when "spotting" cars on industrial spurs. As with other B&O diesels, the Fells Point tractor, shown in November 1981, was painted in blue and gray. *Mike Schafer*

In the 1950s, B&O took delivery of eight Electro-Motive E8s and four E9s, meanwhile rebuilding its EAs and EBs into "E8Ms." Clad in the "sunburst" livery of the early 1960s, E9 1454, stands in the engine terminal of the Michigan Central depot in Detroit in 1963. *Dave Ingles*

12 1937-era EAs and EBs (one EA had been sold to the Alton) into E8s, giving them an "E8m" designation.

As it bought diesel road power from the former steam builders, B&O sampled yard switchers from Lima-Hamilton Corporation, formerly Lima Locomotive Works, buying ten 1,000-hp switchers and 24 1,200-hp models were in 1950 and 1951. By 1952, B&O had enough diesels that it was able to shut down its historic electric operation on the Baltimore Belt. In 1954, the switching operation at Fells Point was also dieselized, but in this case the replacement was a large rubber-tired tractor built by Caterpillar, a manufacturer of construction equipment. A tractor allowed crews to maneuver faster in and out of the tight confines of the neighborhood.

In the early 1950s, railroads were looking for more flexibility in the design of diesel locomotives, and the builders responded by creating a new class of general purpose diesel. The machinery was enclosed in hoods rather than a full-width carbody to improve access for maintenance and allow the locomotive to operate in either direction. B&O's first hood-type diesels were a batch of 13 GP7 road-switchers from EMD in 1953. Other builders also offered hood units, and B&O dabbled with Baldwin and Fairbanks-Morse road-switchers. Less than a dozen Fairbanks-Morse H16-44s were delivered between 1952 and 1957, while a handful of 1,600-hp AS16s came from Baldwin between 1952 and 1955. But B&O's preference for EMD products resulted in much

Running backward with a transfer along the B&OCT near Ash Street in Chicago, new GP30 6949 also wears the sunburst scheme. The GP30s were acquired in 1962–63 to speed up road-freight schedules, so its use in transfer service on this day in 1963 is a little out of the ordinary. *Dave Ingles*

B&O's main diesel shops were at Cumberland, Maryland—also the location of the railroad's principal classification yard. Switchers and road units both are undergoing repairs and maintenance at Cumberland during the later years of the Chessie System era. *Chessie System, collection of William F. Howes Jr.*

larger orders of GP9s through 1958. The railroad also bought six-motor versions of the GP series, the SD7 and SD9—"SD" for special duty—in the mid-1950s. By this time, B&O's motive power department was establishing a standardization program for its diesel locomotives.

B&O took delivery of its last new E-units—four E9s—in 1955. These would be the last new passenger diesels purchased by the B&O, and the E-unit fleet would remain in service until the end of B&O intercity passenger service in 1971. The Fairbanks-Morse road-switchers would be the last new locomotives that B&O would buy that weren't built by Electro-Motive. With the retirement of B&O's last steam locomotive in 1958, dieselization was complete.

THE FINAL GENERATION

The development of the diesel locomotive continued, and more powerful models began to appear in the early 1960s. Baltimore & Ohio purchased 77 GP30 freight locomotives from EMD in 1962 and 1963 to speed up freight

schedules. These were the last new locomotives that an independent B&O would buy.

Although the C&O takeover of 1963 resulted in the introduction of some secondhand C&O diesels to B&O's roster, the B&O did receive new GP35s and six-motor SD35s in 1964 and 1965. EMD introduced the 3,000-hp GP40 in 1965 and its 2,000-hp twin, the GP38, in 1966; the SD40 was also introduced in 1966. Large numbers of GP38s and GP40s were built for B&O in the late 1960s and into the 1970s, and two small groups of SD40s were delivered in 1967 and 1969.

After Chessie System and Seaboard Coast Line Industries merged to form CSX, their locomotive fleets were gradually integrated and the identity of each individual railroad began to disappear from the locomotives in 1987. The last new locomotives to be built for the B&O were 20 3,600-hp SD50 freight locomotives delivered in 1984. The locomotives were painted in the Chessie System scheme and sublettered B&O. Three years later B&O was merged out of existence.

These four brand-new EMD 2,000 hp GP38s have just been delivered to the B&O at Barr Yard in Chicago. They are part of a 50-unit order built in October and November 1967. Twenty more GP38s would come in 1970. *Jim Boyd*

GM50 is a GP40-2 that was painted in a special gold paint scheme to commemorate the 50th anniversary (1922-1972) of locomotive builder Electro-Motive. In July 1984 it was renumbered to 4164 and painted in the standard Chessie scheme. *Collection of Louis A. Marre*

The year 1998 was the dawn of a new age for the remains of the B&O, especially on the west end of the main line to Chicago. In conjunction with the dicing up of Conrail in 1999 by Norfolk Southern and CSX, the former B&O main line to Chicago became one of the most important main lines in the U. S. Conrail traffic on its heavy main line across northern Ohio and Indiana would be split among NS and CSX, and the amount of traffic on the former B&O main would more than double after the split date of June 1, 1999. In 1997–98 this necessitated the complete rebuilding of Willard Yard and the reinstitution of double track west of Deshler to Chicago. On July 25, 1998, the double track is back in at Milford Junction, Indiana, including all new signals. CSX train Q138 has just pounded across the crossing of Conrail's Goshen–Indianapolis main— just like the *New York Trailer Jet* would have 30 years earlier. *David P. Oroszi*

The B&O Legacy

THE SPIRIT OF THE BALTIMORE & OHIO LIVES ON

The company that carried Baltimore & Ohio's name passed into the history books in 1987, but the accomplishments of its employees and management will endure for years to come. The railroad itself continues to function as a vital component of the CSX rail network, while the traditions, memories, and equipment of B&O reside securely in one of the world's finest railroad museums in Baltimore.

BALTIMORE & OHIO RAILS

The Staggers Rail Act of 1980 deregulated the nation's railroads and simplified the process of selling or abandoning unproductive trackage. Chessie System pruned hundreds miles of former B&O track by selling the lines to shortline operators or simply abandoning them. These included portions of the Pittsburgh & Western, Cleveland, Lorain & Wheeling, Cleveland Terminal & Valley, and the Cincinnati, Hamilton & Dayton.

B&O's former Buffalo & Susquehanna and Buffalo, Rochester & Pittsburgh lines were sold to the Genesee & Wyoming, in 1986 and 1988, respectively. The lines now operate as Rochester & Southern and Buffalo & Pittsburgh, part of GWI's family of shortlines.

The two most noteworthy pieces of B&O to disappear from the CSX system were big segments of the Cumberland–St. Louis main line west of Grafton, West Virginia, and much of the Pittsburgh–Wheeling line. CSX rerouted Cumberland–Cincinnati traffic over the Chicago line to Deshler, Ohio, and down the Toledo Division to Cincinnati in 1985. Several segments of the main line between Wilsonburg, West Virginia, and Midland City, Ohio, were sold or abandoned.

But for all the lines that were torn up, many of the ex-B&O routes that CSX retained became more significant in the late 1990s. To secure a better route through Pittsburgh,

CSX purchased 61 miles of Pittsburgh & Lake Erie main line in 1991. B&O had used trackage rights over the P&LE for decades to bypass its own circuitous Pittsburgh & Western. CSX went on to acquire the remainder of P&LE in 1992.

Following the creation of Conrail in 1976, CSX in 1980, and Norfolk Southern in 1982, those three systems dominated the rail network east of the Mississippi River. The situation remained largely unchanged until late 1996 when Conrail announced it would be acquired by CSX, making CSX the largest railroad in the Eastern U. S. Norfolk Southern was not about to let CSX take Conrail without a fight and retaliated with a counter offer to buy Conrail stock.

CSX raised its bid for Conrail and NS matched it. NS then took the matter to court in an attempt to stop the planned merger. The turning point in the battle came in January 1997 when Conrail stockholders voted to take Norfolk Southern's offer into consideration. CSX and NS then entered into negotiations and announced a deal in April 1997 to divide Conrail's assets between themselves. The division of Conrail would give both NS and CSX access to the New York metropolitan area, a market that Conrail had monopolized.

Under the agreement, CSX would take over the former New York Central route from New York through Buffalo to Cleveland. West of Cleveland, NYC's line to Indianapolis and St. Louis would also go to CSX. A new connection was built at Greenwich, Ohio, where the ex-New York Central Cleveland–Indianapolis line crossed B&O's Akron Division. CSX traffic from Boston and New York now uses the new connection to turn west on to the former B&O line. To handle the anticipated increase in business, CSX put back into service the segments of second main track that had been removed from the Pittsburgh–Chicago main line during the 1960s, making this former B&O route one of the most important east of Chicago. Willard Yard was also rebuilt to better handle trains being reclassified for connecting lines at Chicago.

BALTIMORE & OHIO AND AMTRAK

When Amtrak took over the operation of most of the nation's intercity rail passenger services in May 1971, it did not continue operating B&O's remaining passenger trains. B&O commuter service in the Baltimore–Washington, Washington–Brunswick–Martinsburg and Pittsburgh–McKeesport–Versailles corridors continued to be operated by the railroad. However, in September 1971, Amtrak reinstituted passenger service between Washington and Parkersburg, West Virginia. Initially named the *West Virginian* (a former B&O name), it was briefly renamed *Potomac Turbo* when lightweight United Aircraft TurboTrains were used on the run during the spring of 1972. When conventional equipment returned later that year, the schedule took on yet another new name, *Potomac Special*.

The *Potomac Special* was discontinued in May 1973 and replaced with a Washington–Cumberland train called the *Blue Ridge*. In October 1976, Amtrak began operating a new train, the *Shenandoah* (another B&O name) between Washington and Cincinnati, while Amtrak continued to serve the Washing-

ton–Martinsburg run with an abbreviated *Blue Ridge*. The *Shenandoah* ran for five years until the schedule was annulled in 1981 due to financial considerations.

In October 1981, Amtrak rerouted its Chicago–Pittsburgh–Washington service—a leg of the Chicago–New York *Broadway Limited*—off the old Pennsylvania Route via Harrisburg and Port Deposit, Pennsylvania, and moved it to the B&O east of Pittsburgh, resurrecting the name *Capitol Limited* in the process. Initially combined with the *Broadway Limited* west of Pittsburgh, the *Capitol* was made a completely separate schedule in 1986.

In an unusual twist that could only happen in modern-day U.S. passenger railroading, the *Capitol* and *Broadway* were each rerouted off the former PRR line west of Pittsburgh in November 1990. Oddly, the *Broadway* was transferred to B&O's Pittsburgh–Chicago main line—using the twisting Pittsburgh & Western main line to enter downtown Pittsburgh, no less—while the *Capitol* was sent to Cleveland on a former PRR line and thence west over the former NYC to Chicago. The *Broadway* was one of several trains that Amtrak discontinued in September 1995, again due to budget constraints, but Amtrak restored service over the former B&O route between New Castle, Pennsylvania, and Chicago in late 1996 with a new "no frills" version of the *Broadway* known as the *Three Rivers*.